UNLOADED

From Addiction's Self-Destruction to Purpose

JAMIE WEATHERLY

SPARK Publications
Charlotte, North Carolina

UNLOADED

From Addiction's Self-Destruction to Purpose
Jamie Weatherly

Designed, produced, and published by SPARK Publications
SPARKpublications.com
Charlotte, North Carolina

Developmental editing by Sherré DeMao
Photography of Jamie Weatherly by Mark Hanson Photography
Tattoos skillfully created by Kelsea McCree and Family Tradition Tattoo
Stock Image Credits: Agor2012 / Milano M / RedKoala / svekloid / wrathline.labs / shutterstock.com

Printed in the United States of America

Paperback, March 2024, ISBN: 978-1-953555-66-3
Library of Congress Control Number: 2024903557

DEDICATION

The message of this book is dedicated to all those who need it: the suffering, the scared, active and inactive addicts, and their families.

The spirit of this book is dedicated to my two children, OG and Remix. May you never conform, always believe in yourself, never settle, and stay true to who you are.

TABLE OF CONTENTS

SECTION THREE
UNWRAPPING ADDICTION............................... 100

INTRODUCTION

The idea of someone drinking just one or two drinks is mind blowing to me. The notion that someone does just a little bit of a drug, puts away the rest, and saves it for later is completely incomprehensible.

Do it all. Get more. Do it all again. That was me.

I didn't come from a broken home. I didn't endure the hardships of seeing a single parent struggling. My father is a Vietnam vet, a proud University of North Carolina at Chapel Hill graduate, and worked an honest Mecklenburg County career for thirty years. My mom did anything and everything to work around his schedule, my and my sisters' schedules, and still have time to put a dinner on the table. Between the two of them, never a swim meet, soccer game, football game, band competition, dance competition, or whatever activity we three Weatherly kids were involved in was missed. Never. And my parents were not just present, but involved. Coach. Team parent. PTA presidents. Chaperones. Crossing guard. Timers. Starters. Judges. Treasurers. Secretaries. Chauffeurs. Pretty much anything and everything. They were there.

We lived in the same house our whole lives and didn't suffer from any relocation drama. We had the dogs, the fenced-in yard, and an open field across the street to use as my personal playground and football field, which also transformed into my eventual pass-out location. I was Jamie f'n America.

Don't ever think you're too good to be an addict. It happens. It happens for many reasons. I can tell you through my personal experience that part of that formula is placing principles and people into positions of hero when they clearly aren't in line with the life you want to live. I don't blame anything or any person around me as an influence. I blame how in depth I invested myself into them. I was exposed to many of the same things as other people, but I just chose to jump in a lot deeper and lose myself in what wasn't real.

A lot of people confuse crossing the finish line as the victory. The victory is starting the race, whether you finish or not. There are so many people scared or unmotivated to move from the audience to the pool of participants. It doesn't matter what any of these people's opinions might be. It doesn't matter how others are faring in comparison to you.

What matters is that you show up at the starting line and when that starter pistol goes off, you take that first step toward completion. You decide to enter this race of your life to get sober and then live your life the way it was always meant to be. To be the person you were meant to be.

It's only then that you realize how much you will need to unload in the process, and that's when you realize it isn't a race at all. It is your life, waiting to be lived. Truly lived.

THE INSIDE OUT OF ADDICTION

What you see and don't see in yourself is at the core of why and how addiction has such power and control.

❝I had unlocked a forbidden gate in my soul. I was a badass. I was an outlaw. I was the squeaky-clean neighborhood do-good that now has done big boy things.❞

CHAPTER 1

SEEMS HARMLESS

Often addicts will look at their first time using or drinking as the beginning of their struggles. This distorted way of thinking exists because it's easy. It's on the surface. It's diagnosing a symptom, not finding the cause. The reality is that addictive behavior is fed long before any drug is introduced into the body.

Growing up, there had been the initial innocent parental supervised sips. An "Oops I grabbed an opened beer can from the table" moment or two. An annual champagne toast for New Year's as I had gotten older. Innocent on the surface. A sip, or a mere taste, didn't immediately have me committing mail fraud and check forgery, but it did give me an enjoyably sinister feeling.

"I am too young for this."

"I am an outlaw."

"If only my teachers could see this and surely none of my friends were allowed this treachery."

"I am s-p-e-c-i-a-l. No one is like me."

And don't even get me started on the warm, ego-drenching attention I got from such a small postdrink burp. The ball might be dropping at midnight, but this prepubescent dude right here had arrived!

BLAME OR SHAME

From this, one might conclude that my parents and everyone at these holiday parties are to blame for my behaviors and decisions that led me to a life of alcoholism. Roll credits. Thanks for coming out. The book is over.

Quite the contrary.

This behavior bomb was loaded and set to explode regardless of my environment. I was going to put myself through the things I did because my insides were messed up. You can't blame the train tracks when the conductor is batshit crazy.

NO SELF-CONTROL

The first time I ever got drunk was at an end-of-season party for the neighborhood pool. I had taken a supervised sip or two from a parental cocktail, even had two beers at a "parents are out of town" house party, but never been full-blown drunk. Until all the lifeguards got together.

To be clear, I was a concession-stand attendee, not quite old enough to be a whistle twirler. However, I was "family" and found myself at this shindig, and I also found myself with a twelve-pack of Bud Dry. Bud Dry was chosen because a few weeks earlier I overheard a neighborhood hero, someone I had always looked up to and deemed cool by my standards, telling some stories with his friends and mentioning this was his drink of choice. So, naturally it had to be mine as well, and I needed to come equipped to impress.

In the span of a couple hours, I had made my way through eleven of the twelve beers. Being that we all knew each other and had been friends for a few years, this wasn't a party of getting acquainted. I was barely old enough to drive, and the rest of the staff ranged in age from their twenties through the beginning of their thirties. I now spoke to the older folks with a new confidence. I cussed. I insulted. I felt taller. I felt heard. I felt like I belonged. I felt equal. I also felt a nasty carpet burn as I fell down the steps and puked all over myself. One of the mother hens took care of me, force-fed me water, and propped me on a pile of pillows so I wouldn't Jimi Hendrix myself. I passed out.

The next day, despite the headache and blackout from my overindulgence, I felt good. A new, more paralleled relationship with the older coworkers had been forged. I felt in control. I had unlocked a forbidden gate in my soul. I was a badass. I was an outlaw. I was the squeaky-clean neighborhood do-good that now has done big boy things. I thought, "I'm a man now."

During my junior and senior years of high school, hanging out on the weekends became more and more important. All plans, however, had to include at least alcohol. Eventually weed was introduced and became more prevalent. But no matter what, the plans had to include drinking.

In my neighborhood, I had two best friends. I am fortunate that to this day we still are friends. In the hood, we would score drinks and just drive around aimlessly if there was nothing to do. We'd hear of a house party someone from the school was throwing, and there was always the occasional hotel party. If someone's parents were out for the night or working late, we'd show up at that house for a while. Being we were still in school, we had a respectable curfew, usually midnight or so, and we would always honor it. By appearing obedient, we could get away with more.

I also had a larger circle of friends on a different side of town, about a twenty-five- to thirty-minute drive. These kids lived in bigger houses, had nicer cars, and went to newer schools. These were my friends from the national swim team.

Many times my neighborhood friends would come along, but usually I'd ride solo to hang with my crosstown friends. That was the real escape. That's when I could immerse myself in a totally different crowd. It was acceptable to cruise to a local spot and hang out in the parking lot. There were also more frequent house parties. I didn't know most of these people. Most of them didn't know me. I was allowed to be whoever I wanted. I could lie. I could shift personalities. Hell, I could even dress in ways I never did. I could fit in or stick out. I was a prep, a thug, a hood, a scholar, a genius, and a dopehead all at once. Whenever I wanted, whatever I wanted. It was a freedom that felt so good.

Harmless, right? Just a normal kid going through normal things. Testing boundaries. Being drawn to the forbidden out of youthful curiosity. Just a rebellious phase.

For most, yes. For the developing brain of an addict, this is defining the blueprint of future relationships and self-worth for years to come. Play the role of what it is your audience wants. I am here to entertain and be the center of the party, regardless of whether it is my genuine personality or I need to fabricate one. When feeling uncomfortable, run. No need for truths. No need for amends. There's always a willing crowd to supply the attention you crave. Don't plant roots. Stay mobile. Like a nomad of personalities, it is best to have many safe havens instead of one genuine home. I want all the love, all the attention, all the success, all the controversy, all the credit, and all the victories. The least amount of work I have to put forth, the better. The least amount of people that know I am merely a scared child trying to find my way, the better.

Harmless right? Nah. Fully equipping an addict soldier for his war with himself.

❝ I was drinking not just for the obsession I had with the buzz but also for the obsession I had with the attention. ❞

CHAPTER 2

CENTER OF ATTENTION

High school continued. Senior year was much of the same, with weekend blackouts and finding excuses to drink during the week. Lying to my parents to cover it up. Lugging stupid amounts of bottle caps in my backpack because people would think I was oh so awesome. My natural, pubescent ego was also hulking up at this time. Big man on campus. Senior year meant a light at the end of the tunnel and getting out of here. Senior athlete in the pool. I was also growing in my asshole-ishness and being more and more of a distraction and a detriment to myself.

I had the opportunity to go to the University of North Carolina at Chapel Hill, where my father and his father went. Growing up, I thought I surely would too. I also could've gone to North Carolina State, Davidson, and possibly even Duke and many other local, well-respected universities because I made the academic cut.

I was a swimmer and wanted to continue swimming through college. That was my plan. Good in my own right, a shining star on a neighborhood and high school level, pretty dang okay on a regional level, yet unheard of nationally.

I would've probably been allowed to practice with the aforementioned schools but would more than likely never get wet at a meet.

Then I was introduced to NCAA Division III schools.

The schools that I looked at in this division put much more emphasis on the *student* in student athlete than the *athlete*. Don't get me wrong, I wanted a college education, but the allure of my worth in the pool for these schools was way more attractive to me. One school in particular caught my attention. Goucher College reached out to me. The swim coach was interested, and although they didn't offer athletic scholarships, I could score an academic one. All it took was one quick tour of the campus, an overnight stay with a guy named Grossman, and a glimpse at the pool scoreboard to see I could already beat quite a few of the school records to securely lure me in.

BIG FISH, LITTLE POND

I was going to be a Gopher damn it, not because I wanted to, but because I could start my collegiate swimming career at the top of the food chain. Addict thinking y'all. Why work hard and challenge yourself when mediocrity and complacency can give you immediate results? There's an undeniable cliched metaphor here about the size of an aquatic animal relative to the size of its environment, but this is bigger than any pond-bound fish. I was heading north to be the baddest mf'er this team and its conference had ever seen.

The first time ever meeting many of my teammates was at a beginning-of-semester party. Propped against the wall in one of the dorms was a sign of the "unofficial" team logo and mascot, the Goucher Gators. Apparently, the college's board of trustees frowned upon the swim team having its separate mascot and all signage was removed. A few swimmers held on to their outlawed "Gator" swim caps, and my teammates who were also roommates, Mangold and Jacoby, scored the marquee sign. There were a few signatures on the sign, a few names I recognized as some of the folks I had met. Even the coach's scribble was on it. I was presented with a Sharpie. In all my blazing naive glory, I signed "Jamie (better than everyone else) Weatherly" without giving it any thought. What an insufferable prick move. Though I didn't think so at the time, I realize it for what it was now.

SCHOOL SUCCESS

Freshman year of college was an all-around success in all the categories worth my measure. I overcame the fear and unknown of living ten hours and a few states away from home. I excelled in academics, especially the first semester, making the dean's list.

Per my own expectations, I ruled the pool. I won a conference championship in the 400 individual medley—a race that concluded with a come-from-behind victory, winning by a tenth of a second, besting a defending champ, and beating his conference record. It was a storied race that Hollywood couldn't contrive. Michael Phelps stole my schtick. I was the original exciting, partying, swimming star, damn it! And the friends and good times far exceeded my optimistic drunken desires.

Notice I mentioned dean's list *first* semester? My partying reality began to set in as the year swam on.

Returning for my sophomore year, I was happy to continue where I had left off. Partying. Exploiting myself. Swimming. Partying. Having a class of students below me that I could look so cool for. Partying. And school stuff.

BIGGER FISH

My sophomore year coincided with the transfer of a local hero to our small school. The worst thing that could ever happen to the large-aquatic-monster hero of our story occurred when a bigger fish showed up to the humble, small little fishing hole.

Picture a small-town Brad Pitt entering the frame with the coolest Oakley sunglasses as a paraphrased Bradley Nowell sings "everything was going fine until the day he met me."

Originally from the Baltimore suburbs, Paxton had decided to come home and not return to Arizona State University. A fellow swimmer, we were introduced within hours of him hitting the campus. He found his way to the dorm now shared by Mangold and me, and we spent the next couple days before classes testing the boundaries of sanity. We had a lot in common, including the desire to outdo each other.

On the surface I loved Paxton. To this day he is still a valued friend of mine. But we have been through hell— through hell together and through hell because of each other. The growth we endured because of and despite each other is deserving of its own book. Hell, its own Netflix series. But to focus here, Paxton was a threat to my very existence. I loved him. I hated him.

Paxton was a faster swimmer than me. Paxton was taller than me. Paxton sang louder to cooler songs than I did.

Paxton's car was faster than mine. Paxton was brasher. He was brighter. He was flashier. If I had ever done three, he had done six. If I had fractured this, he had broken all these. It was as if my super-ego itself was personified. I saw standing before me the embodiment of everything I thought I was, and now everything I wanted to be. And my competition would ultimately destroy me.

Not only was Paxton the life of the party, he had focused, purpose-driven goals with his education. He knew exactly what he wanted to be when he grew up. I was fish-flopping my way through a psychology major. Although thoroughly entertained by the classes, I had no drive, extra interest, or career-minded direction.

I had to up my game. I had to party harder. I had to fall harder. I had to soar. I had to crash. I had to screw up. I had to overcome. I put myself through a myriad of torturous roller-coaster rides to keep my reputation at the level I thought it should be and guess what. No one gave a damn! The day I realized I wasn't nearly as important to everyone else's daily life was a day another shackle was removed. Unfortunately, this lesson was years away from being learned.

Don't get me wrong, Paxton and I got along swimmingly. We were peas in a pod, man. Thick as thieves. He knows my mom and dad and has met my important Charlotte, North Carolina, friends, and I've met his. He came to Charlotte for my twenty-first birthday and a group of about twenty of us went to see Rage Against the Machine and Wu-Tang Clan. We didn't go small in any way, ever.

It wasn't until years removed that I realized I was holding him as close to me as possible to not only attempt to dim his shine but to steal as much residual attention as I could. I was in a competition, deeply invested, and absolutely no one else was paying it any attention. Through years of clarity, I realized that it wasn't Paxton that I hated; it was myself. I just used him as my resentment muse. Had he never ventured into my safe little pond, I would've found someone else. It's a reoccurring theme with me and countless others that struggle with all forms of addiction. No matter where you go, there *you* are.

ATTENTION AT ANY COST

Looking back now, I realize during these years I was drinking not just for the obsession I had with the buzz but also for the obsession I had with the attention. The buzz though, was always achievable. It was a guarantee. The attention, however, wasn't. That's what fueled my fire to continue, to increase, and to do more and more and more.

Through the college years, the years after, and the restaurant years, through the blurs and the crystal clear memories, through the fortunes and self-created devastations, I was always striving to be "it"—the one who everyone else wanted to be like.

I heard one of my own falsely elevated heroes Ric Flair quip, "all the women want to be with me, all the men want to be like me." This is an honest insight to what I was striving for and how I felt I was viewed. And when that became threatened, I didn't change. Why would I change?

This master plan was flawless. I would turn up the volume. More of this. Throw money that way. Bring people in.

A good idea in life is to surround yourself with those that are going to bring out the best in you. Those that are who you want to emulate. Well, I tried, and those folks weren't responding as I felt they should. By my merit or their own, a lot of those people went away.

I found myself constantly replacing my circle with people of less integrity, of less value to my life. But the further down I went, the easier it was to get the responses I craved. My directions were followed, and the script was playing out.

A true friend will ask you if you're okay and be genuinely concerned with your answer. When you are among the dirtiest of the dirties, and you're just as covered in soot but delusionally believe you're better than and in charge, you won't be told no. Your motives won't be questioned. Your well-being isn't a consideration.

At one point, I found myself in the back of a car in a dark alley, taking bumps of what I presumed to be cocaine off a dirty EBT card with two guys I'd just met. My friend who drove was up front with his loaded gun. None of them asked, "Hey Jamie, what are some of your lifetime goals?"

But man, I'm sure they thought I was a bad, bad dude.

"You have to feel the hole to fill the hole. It takes awareness and an unveiling of the belligerent denial that is occurring."

CHAPTER 3

A
GAPING HOLE

Imagine coming up to a massive hole in the ground. Beside it are giant piles of dirt, obviously way more than needed to fill the hole. If it was your job to fill the hole, no questions asked, it would be most proper to pick a pile and shovel it in. You wouldn't waste your time trying to figure out how the hole got there in the first place. You would just focus on the solution.

So goes the recovery process at times.

This is a guided process. It seems simple enough. Fill the hole. You have to fill this hole with the "dirt" provided by those attempting to help you. Don't bring or offer your own dirt. Don't be lured by this pile of bigger rocks a few steps closer. Attempting to occupy this hole with the wrong substance, with the wrong answers, or with misdirected spiritual journeys will leave it empty. That's just cleaning up and moving a mess from one spot to another. No progress is made. Nothing gets filled. The hole is still there, gaping even more.

What is the gaping hole in their spirit that makes an addict drown themselves in false realities?

Childhood trauma. Learned behavior. A yearning to escape. A need for acceptance. Inferiority issues. Confidence issues—not just a lack of but also an overabundance.

UNMET EXPECTATIONS

We have a vision of what we expect "normal" to be; expectations about how the world and its people should treat us and respond to us. We find more often than not that those expectations aren't met. We don't get what we want. And a lot of times boozing and using gives us the comfort we are looking for in a world that is not cooperating.

We can create our own world, eliminating who we want and choosing its population. We form our own rules. We set our own standards. We don't live in the reality around us but manipulate a bizzaro land where we are right and anyone to doubt that shall be damned.

Along the way, we can encounter others that have created similar narratives. This is comforting because it proves we have been correct all along. We have been mistreated, we deserve more, things just aren't fair, we never get a break. There is a feeling that you have found company that supports you.

We might make so many "rules" that no one dares venture in. So distraught with society, we have made ourselves the outcast. We rationalize further hatred of people that we determined weren't worthy of our world for not trying to come into our world.

We create all our boundaries. We build all our walls. We separate ourselves socially from friends, family, and coworkers. We put ourselves on a secluded island by our own choices, behaviors, habits, and views and then curse the world for leaving us alone.

So goes the ridiculous cycle. The only comfort is in escaping sobriety, and these escapes are how we believe we are filling our hole. We are in the personal hells of our own making. We are angered, we escape. We are scared, we escape. The escape becomes the only reality we are comfortable in, and therefore we must continue to create situations that rationalize it. We cause trouble. We become negligent. We ignore friends. We let go of enjoyed pastimes and hobbies. And we curse them all for not being there. So, we drink or use again, staying loaded and keeping the hole empty.

As an addict in recovery we are never done. Resentments, regrets, and blown opportunities haunt us. These leeches on our psyche can direct our thoughts and motivate our moods for years, sober or not. It always seems to come down to fear. A healthy fear is rational. It can in fact save our lives at times. But an addict lets fear control them. Fear of missing out. Fear of being left behind. Fear of failure. Hell, even fear of success. Fear of disappointing themselves or their loved ones. Again, these are all fears that a lot of "normals" might have, but to an addict's mind, these are crippling obsessions.

Sometimes you figure out the hole, the cause of it. Sometimes you're advised not to. Some never figure it out or even try. The fact is there is a hole, and it needs to be filled.

Filling the hole is a constant pursuit. It's a yearning for something different or for more of what we have. There are times when it isn't even the destination we have in mind so much as it is the chase.

You have to *feel* the hole to fill the hole. It takes awareness and an unveiling of the belligerent denial that is occurring. Feel the hole. Fill the hole. Eventually, you can feel whole.

" Addicts are neck deep in addiction and fear consumes them. Outrun lies. Outrun overlapping stories. Outrun accountability. **"**

CHAPTER 4

CHASING SOMETHING

Before the blackout of the lifeguard party, I found myself one Friday night at an after-party for one of our high school football games. It was super awesome because although I made sure to be the center of attention of my immediate social circle in school, this was totally expanding into circles I had yet to tread. Much cooler kids were in the mix—like the longhairs that smoke and skip class or dudes with full beards and the girls that look like women. This was big time.

We walked into the house—not sure whose it was, but it was in my neighborhood—and not an adult was in sight, just wall-to-wall juniors and seniors from the high school. I was with an older friend and was greeted by a handful of people that knew me as "the fast swimmer kid." It was like one of those crazy teen movies where more and more people came in carrying cases of beer. It was a different time, man. You walked into a convenience store with a little confidence and a little more facial hair, and you could have whatever you wanted. No questions asked.

This story doesn't end in felonious debauchery, sorry to disappoint. My friend actually had his girlfriend with him and she had the same midnight curfew as I did, which is why I was allowed out. He was my ride because I wasn't driving yet.

I had two beers. On the drive back, I felt a little more talkative than usual but otherwise normal. I got home, got to bed, and was up in time early Saturday morning for swim practice.

FOOLING SELF

There was nothing spectacular about this practice. We did the usual, and I caught a ride to that Saturday's designated unofficial team breakfast. My boy ChiefDaddy was driving and there was another teammate, Tammie, in the car. We were discussing the absence of a teammate from practice that day.

"He probably went to a party and had too much to drink," was one of the proposed reasons.

Then, I, with all the world's experience of going to one unsupervised high school party, put on my big boy pants and spewed gospel.

"That's bullshit. He should know better if that's the case. He knew he had practice this morning. I mean, I went to a party last night and had a few beers, but I knew when to stop."

Okay. We all know "a few" was two. We also know that the only reason I left this party when I did was because my ride home was leaving the party. We all know that now, but my two friends in the car that morning didn't.

This made me feel some kind of way, boy I tell ya. *This* is the feeling. My friends had to think I was so smart, so in control. A rebel of sorts, a badass, and at the same time tough enough to show up for an early morning practice. This is what I assumed they believed, so it had to be the truth. I felt important, smart, and wise. This put me on a pedestal because, you know, I'm a responsible experienced drinker. I know how to separate partying and responsibilities. I'm better than.

I needed more of this feeling.

CHASE IS ON

Fast-forward to June 3, 1994. The calendar says it was a Friday. I was wearing a suit under my cap and gown, and I know I had a case of Bud Ice hidden under the sweet sheepskin seat covers of my little Honda.

I don't remember many more details of that day, except the speech delivered by one of my fellow seniors, Jennifer Stewart—in particular, the part about the mighty Serengeti. It's an old parable I've run across from time to time and like to share with people. It's good motivation for athletes, for the work setting, and for students at graduation.

Here's how it goes if you haven't heard it before: Every morning as the sun rises across the Serengeti, the gazelles awaken. Each gazelle knows for that day they must outrun the fastest of lions or they will never see another sunrise. Under that same sun the mighty lions also arise. Each lion knows for that day they must outrun the slowest gazelle or they will not eat.

The point is, be you a lion or a gazelle, when the sun comes up your ass better be running.

It's a call of action to get going. Move forward or die. Get to fighting or get to running, but no matter what, get to gettin'.

I have received this message a little differently as time has passed. It is true, we must run. Never stop learning. Never stop improving. Never stop running. But why do you choose to run? Are you a gazelle? Are you running out of fear of dying? Are you running because you are being chased? Are you running because another force, another being, dictates your run?

Or are you a lion? You run to eat. You want to eat more and more. You run for life quality. You run for dominance. You run to preserve your pride.

Gazelle running is running as an addict, but it's not exclusive to addicts. It is complacent running. Running because you know no better. Running because you are the self-imposed hunted. Running to merely get by or to simply survive. Doing just enough and looking over your shoulder to make sure you are okay. You quit running when you believe you are safe.

Lion running is running to move forward. Chasing goals. Taking care of yourself and others. It is running to rip flesh, not running to keep yours from being ripped. You quit running when you are done or until you need to prey again.

So, indeed, when that sun comes up, you'd better be running. But now, for me, it isn't about whether you are a gazelle or a lion. The gazelle runs not knowing when the run is ending. A gazelle wakes and thinks, "Oh, crap. Here we go again." Addicts do the gazelle run. Addicts are neck-deep in addiction and fear consumes them. Outrun lies. Outrun overlapping stories. Outrun accountability. Outrun realizing personal potential. Outrun anything remotely shiny that could give off the faintest of reflections forcing you to see yourself. Falsely busy. Defensively scurrying. Don't answer the phone. Don't agree to help with friends and family. Don't make any commitments. Just run out of fear.

The lion runs and decides when the run is over. For me, it is the run of a lion or it is no run at all. It's that endless chase. Feast or famine, it is up to the lion. But are you chasing your dreams or chasing your tail?

❝Peer pressure doesn't cause addiction. It can, however, be the lit match needed to ignite the stockpiled gasoline-soaked kindling.❞

CHAPTER 5

COMPETING WITH SELF

We beings are by nature a strong, bullheadedly stubborn breed. We often do things way beyond what would scare off the status quo. Sometimes we do this out of a self-created need. Sometimes we excel out of spite for expected failure. But as we explore the importance of self-worth, we must also look at the competition we have at times with our biggest ally and our biggest, most detrimental enemy.

That f'n person looking back at us from the mirror? *That* is our most inescapable rival.

SELF-PRESSURE

Peer pressure can pop the bottle for many. People we deem as "friends" would never challenge our loyalty or character because of any decisions or choices we make. That's an easy conclusion to make when we are sane and wise. In the midst of growing up and finding ourselves, we are seldom sane and wise, and even less both sane and wise at the same time.

I am adamant that peer pressure doesn't cause addiction. It can, however, be the lit match needed to ignite the stockpiled, gasoline-soaked kindling. Peer pressure can cause us to use. It is the addiction living in us that will cause us to use again and again and again.

Peer pressure is a real thing, but most of mine came through my own creation. No one ever said to me, "Here do this!" However, I saw people I deemed as cool perform certain behaviors and I yearned for their status. My peer pressure was more self-pressure from my screwed-up perception of my peers.

I created my peer pressure. Though it wasn't obvious to those around me, I was in constant pursuit to outdo. To match. To mimic. To elicit the same response. I expected the same results, the same laughs, the same acceptance, and the same credibility. There was no competition and no one was keeping score. Yet, I was determined to beat everyone at being themselves. I wanted to surpass everyone. I wanted to please everyone. I wanted to *be* everyone.

I witnessed schoolmates, teammates, neighborhood friends, or whoever I thought was cool acting in certain ways. Then I would mimic that behavior, be it a loud stereo, a clothing brand, or ultimately drinking and drugging. I was in awe of these people. They were, in fact, the stars or heroes of my immediate social circle. Not celebrities, not larger-than-life entities, but the coolest guys on the street. The loudest guy in the dorm. The most popular this or that. Little did I know that not only was the pedestal I was putting these people on nonexistent, but everyone else around me wasn't handing out the keys to the socialite kingdom I sought to be in.

I just assumed everyone thought like me. I projected my emotions, my opinions, my thoughts, and my priorities on everyone around me. And, boy howdy, it pissed me off when people didn't react the way I thought they should have. If we all laughed at this joke by that guy, then you surely will enjoy the joke by me. If an act was done for attention, a clout grab if you will, then surely I can match or outdo the act. Surely I'll receive the same admiration, or I will perform it again and again until either my audience gives me the reaction they are supposed to or I find an audience that responds accordingly.

I didn't have much peer pressure. I had "me pressure." I would be influenced by the things around me I saw as cool or cutting edge, but it was my need to take them to the next level that drove me. There was no "Here take this or do this if you wanna hang out with us."

BE EVERYONE AND NO ONE

I had a desire to be everything I saw as cool, to own everything I saw as cool, and to speak and act in the ways I thought were cool. It all came from within. I remember this thought process while very young—thinking I was indeed the center of *everyone's* focus.

I modified the way I walked through a corridor in kindergarten because I *knew* everyone was looking at me, and I tried to emulate the movements I had seen a super rad first grader do.

A fistfight broke out in the fourth grade over a kickball game because I couldn't fathom this kid from the opposite team disagreeing with me. It was as if he was telling me the sky was red. I was ready to kill and/or die that day. I had to be right, and I had to be center stage. I would not be embarrassed or even questioned.

This continued through middle school and high school, a personal torment I was putting myself through daily. Don't even get me started on how long I would spend getting every single hair in place. You'd think I was modeling. And boy was I ever mad when *Beverly Hills 90210* was a hit and my sideburns weren't ready to grow yet. It was a status symbol I couldn't achieve and it was infuriating.

The result was that I was constantly beating myself up over these series of statuses, these points to go on a nonexistent scoreboard for a game that no one else was aware that they were playing. Now entering the game for the home team, number 8 on my jersey but number one in my heart, Alcohol! This certainly will help.

With the early drinking came the early drinking and driving. I mostly restricted my alcohol use to the weekends while in high school, but it was a constant obsession during the week. I had in my head the way I should be received, the way those around me should respond, and the exalted awe all should have. And once again, not everyone was reading from my script.

I was constantly finding myself in a competition with a whole bunch of people that didn't know there was a competition going on. Who knows the rhyme or reason why some people like broccoli and some don't? There's no logic behind that. But for the things I liked, the things I deemed as cool, the things I was interested in, I had to outdo anyone in sight.

To sum up a common narrative of the movie version of Chuck Palahniuk's *Fight Club*, I was endlessly pursuing things I didn't need, things at times I didn't even want, in the vain attempt to outdo, outshine, and outspend people who weren't even paying attention to me. Sometimes these were actual friends, and sometimes they were mere acquaintances I spied on from the shadows. I would curse them, wish them failure, keep tally on a nonexistent scoreboard of where I stood against them. I would have to acquire more.

Do more. Be more. This carried over from material possessions into substance abuse.

Oh, you wanna see a real f-up? Watch this.

"The checklist of things desired is endless and the masks necessary to chase them are countless."

CHAPTER 6

NEVER ENOUGH

I have a very irrational fear that I am not going to have enough. It's like impending doom. I worry that I will not have enough food, clothes, light bulbs ... anything and everything. I've never gone to bed hungry or not known where the next meal was coming from. I've never gone without and always managed to get more than needed of whatever I've wanted, but I'm still apprehensive that I won't have enough.

When I buy food, be it at a restaurant or at your local grocer, I take in for a meal what can easily feed three grown adults. When I need two of something I will buy five or six. I keep twisty ties, hoard emails, and save broken gadgets. I have stacks of shoes, shirts, socks, and even more socks that are yet to be worn. Many things are still in the original packaging and with retail labels and stickers, just waiting for the right time to be used. What that time is I do not know, but I will be prepared.

This obsession, this compulsion—it's all related to addiction. There is so much more to this disorder than intaking mind-altering substances. It's an uneasiness with the world. It's trying to control and micromanage your own little universe. It's having anxiety that, when there is nothing to be anxious over, causes more anxiety.

It's part of that hole that I try to fill.

To this day, years sober, I try to pack my "character hole" full of unnecessary abundance—garbage, name brands, gluttony—all to keep me occupied and distract me from reality.

A WALKING CONTRADICTION

The reality is that I am both normal and f-ed up. I am rational and insane. I can be cold and warmly emotional. I am everything. And sometimes I need to hide it. Hide it from the world and hide it from myself.

I need to make sure I have enough. More than enough.

The year 1993 saw the arrival of Zima, a sparkling malt beverage that tasted like a generic lemon-lime soda. It was crystal clear and had a slightly higher-than-beer alcohol content. The best part? It was odorless and not all our teachers were hip to this new product, so we saw it as a green light to drink in school. Couldn't get enough of Zima!

Whether hanging with local neighborhood friends or trekking across town for swim teammates' parties, overindulgence and self-control was never a thought.

Around my sophomore year of high school, smoking weed came into play. At first I never really felt anything, then this one time weed had me stuck within the cushions of the couch. I was hearing everyone around me, was having coherent thoughts, but was completely mute and immobile. This lasted a few hours and eventually functionality returned. And like a good addict in the making, I repeated this behavior a few more times at a few more weekend outings until, eventually, I figured it out: couldn't get enough of that weed either.

MORE, MORE, MORE

I became brazen with my drinking and smoking. I'd keep the empty cases of beer boxes in my trunk for a few weeks as if they were a bountiful treasure. I'd pull up to the trash can at the front of the school, pop the trunk, and unload five, six, seven, or eight empty boxes of Budweiser, Bud Ice, Natty Light, and whatever else I had amassed. An empty tequila, vodka, or grain alcohol bottle. A smorgasbord of libations. With my swimming buddies there would be empty malt liquor bottles, because I was hood and gangsta and that's what I drank.

Never having enough takes on many facets. The checklist of things desired is endless and the masks necessary to chase them are countless. The constant pursuit of things is a trick we play on ourselves to keep from focusing on what is really important. Our family, our finances, and our physical and mental health all take a back seat to the pursuit.

Let me do this. Let me go here. Let me acquire these. Let me overconsume, overcompensate, and overspend as long as I don't have to settle and figure out the biggest riddle—who I am.

" While I walked among the 'normal,' I painfully bent and stretched my personality into what I thought those around me wanted it to be. **"**

CHAPTER 7

IDENTITY CRISIS

There was a gaping abyss in my soul that formed around the idea that I had no idea who I was, no idea who I wanted to be, and no idea which direction to look for answers. I had an identity crisis.

I wanted to please everyone, yet I wanted to be an outsider at the same time. The flaw in this plan was not everyone had the allure toward the outsider that I did. While I walked among the "normal," I painfully bent and stretched my personality into what I thought those around me wanted it to be. I wanted approval from everyone. I wanted to be cool. I wanted to be feared. I wanted to be admired. I wanted everything and anything, and I was so busy trying to balance this house of cards I couldn't even figure out who I really was.

I based all my interests on those around me. If I saw a crowd admiring some dude's loud stereo, then I needed a loud stereo to get that admiration. If I saw envy in classmates' eyes toward someone with expensive shoes or name-brand clothes, then I needed those clothes. I would remember clever quips I heard at school and try to fly them as my own at swim practice. I would claim to be this person that liked this music and had this opinion, then go to another group and claim the counterpoints to my alter ego. I would at times lose myself, forgetting which script I was supposed to be reading from.

BETWEEN DRUNKS AND HIGHS

Alcohol helped, boy did it ever. It removed the restraints and allowed me to be free. Not honestly and courageously free, though. Essentially, it allowed me to ride the roller coaster without the safety harness. It was a freedom from caring, concern, or integrity. At this point, those character traits didn't matter. What mattered was the never-ending marathon *that I had created myself* to achieve acceptance by all. With the libations running through me, I could speak freely. Let the bulldog mouth override the puppy dog ass. Preach expertise on things I knew nothing about. Argue for the sake of the argument, often flipping sides of the debate from one day to the next. Dance freely. Fight relentlessly. Fear nothing. The superpowers were still there from the lifeguard party years prior. I felt taller, faster, and better looking. I was fully loaded and unstoppable.

Fast-forward to a year into the restaurant industry and life was good. I had grown comfortable in my new normal as it also let me keep the lifestyle of my old normal. I needed something to do between drunks and highs. It once was school and swim meets, but now I had a job *that paid me* to pass time between chases.

The pay thing was key. I was living at home and by the grace of my overloving and enabling parents I had no bills. I had to put gas in my ultra sweet Honda CRX for my six-mile round trip to and from work. I could buy all the shoes and clothes (this was heavy into my Hilfiger phase) I wanted, score all the dope I could find, and run up all the bar tabs I wanted to. Essentially, it was like my last three semesters of college but with a paycheck. Yet never enough.

As much as I spent, it all went to frivolous wants and no real needs. I had graduated from a couple pairs of old corduroys to three or four classic houndstooth checkered chef pants that someone gave me. I was still working in a pair of old, beat-up Timbs that had a couple visible holes. That changed after a lesson from Craig, one of the kitchen managers I was working under at the time and someone I deeply respected and admired.

Him: "Bro, you look like shit."

Me: "What do you mean?"

Him: "Your pants are too big and you have duct tape on your boots. What's wrong with you?"

I was befuddled because I was being personally attacked by my hero here and, technically, I was compliant with the work uniform policy. My new-to-me chef pants were indeed "official chef pants," so they passed. My boots were black, minus the duct tape band-aids. I had completely adhered to the handbook's descriptions. There was no mention of the *condition* of your uniform.

Craig affirmed, "You need some boots. Some boots that are *work* boots, not your hip-hop wannabe boots. You need to take pride in what you look like. Your image, believe it or not, is important. You can be the baddest dude here but if you look like shit, you will be treated like shit." And to make sure I heard him the first time: "Bro, you look like shit."

DECEIVING APPEARANCES

This had never occurred to me. While not working, I had all the fly gear. Shoes and hats would match. Never cross brands; always Nike or always Adidas, but never a little of both. I can't stand scuffed kicks. I purposely won't wear white shirts because I can't keep them clean. But my work attire? Slop. Shameless, sometimes unwashed slop. The chef coats and chef hats were switched out with our linen company so the top half wasn't an issue, but from waist down I was a bum. I didn't even realize it, but bro ... I looked like shit.

Craig's "you're going to receive the treatment you look like you deserve" lesson was on a Friday. A payday Friday to be more exact. Keep in mind this was "way back" in the 1900s. Unless you were a big-time banker or corporate executive, direct deposit was a concept you'd see on *Lifestyles of the Rich and Famous*. We still received a *paycheck* that we would take to a *bank* and exchange it for *cash*. One step above cave drawings, I tell ya.

The timing of this lesson was around eight in the evening. I had completed my mid shift and Craig was closing. True to the big brother to all that he really was, he didn't just point out a problem, he suggested a solution.

"Look," he said as he pulled up his pants leg. "See these? These are from [big commercial retail store that used to be open 24 hours a day]. Go get you a pair right now. In fact," he continued, reaching into his pocket and pulling out a hundred dollar bill, "get me a pair too."

I took the five-minute drive to the Mart that has Walls. I found my size and scored Craig's as well. I returned to the restaurant proud both of the personal errand and of upping my work image. Craig gave his approval, let me keep the change, and warned me to never let myself look like a bum. It was the first of many "goose and the golden egg" lessons I would encounter.

These learning experiences weren't concretely embedded in my head immediately, but they were never forgotten.

I was loading my database with life lessons. I just wasn't 100% ready to live by them yet.

THE OUTSIDE IN OF ADDICTION

How others see you and relate to you is in direct proportion to how you relate to them and how you want them to see you.

"I intentionally kept separating myself from the pack and then had gut-wrenching pains when I wasn't accepted."

CHAPTER 8

BUILDING WALLS

Growing up in suburbatopia, I wasn't necessarily required to listen to Willie Nelson and The Beatles, but I really reached out to find ways to relate to West Coast gangster rap. This genre was hot and had many talented performers and producers. I couldn't just listen to it as a musical piece; I wanted to live it. Yep, "never enough" showing up again. So far removed as a gangster of any kind, I strived to live and identify with the words of NWA and, later on, Tupac and the solo works of Ice Cube and many others.

A big factor in this was a lot of my contemporaries, like my schoolmates and swim team friends, were *not* listening to this music. I was so determined not to be like everyone else. Why? Not sure. Maybe by being a tad bit different, I wouldn't be held to expectant norms. To hear "that's just the way he is" or "that's just Jamie" gave me the greatest sense of relief. By making myself intentionally different, I felt I had been allotted my own set of rules.

I was scared of success more than failure. I didn't want to put myself in a situation where I would suffer a defeat of any kind. I would play it safe. Put myself places I shouldn't be. Build false relationships geared toward ego-driven profit. I would claim a false uniqueness to not just separate myself from "all the others" but to separate myself from *me*. I didn't want people to know the truth—that I was normal. I had dreams, fears, and hopes and things I liked, loved, hated, and didn't know about. The "normal" scared me. My own honest thoughts scared me. Hiding behind so many "fake mes" to please (in my mind at least) whichever crowd I was hanging out with was easier.

What scared me the most? Being me and trying to understand this person looking at me in the mirror. It was easier just to be someone, anything else.

JAIL WALLS

I was so concerned with creating a false narrative of who I was that I built a persona of beliefs, ethics, and bravado that were all contrived. I intentionally kept separating myself from the pack and then had gut-wrenching pains when I wasn't accepted.

For ten years, I would find myself in a revolving door of self-imposed hell that never slapped me in the face like it should have. Until Debbie.

After one of my many downward swoops, I found myself living back at my mom and dad's house. I entered an outpatient drug dependency program. I had no intention of changing my life or decision-making process but figured if I could get through this program and get a nice little certificate, it would look good in front of my inevitable judge.

Court came. I was called as the first case and was berated as if I were being tried for murder and had been caught red-handed. My charges were indeed serious, but the judge was taking full advantage of the situation and employing his own version of a scared straight presentation. He was slamming his hand on his bench, papers were flying, his face reddening with every justified insult thrown my way. He sentenced me to five years in prison and as my knees buckled and I began to black out, he slammed his fist down again. He screamed, continuously increasing his volume, that he would suspend the sentence with a myriad of probationary requirements. He concluded with stating that if he ever even remotely thought he smelled me walk through the courthouse doors, I would be locked up for those five years.

Life continued on, pretty much repeating similar events. I'd land in a good chunk of trouble and manage to keep my nose clean for the duration of any probation periods. City to city, it just kept happening.

This continued ad nauseam for years and I found myself, yet again, in front of a judge. His menu of probation fares included completing a mandatory outpatient rehab program. It just happened to be the exact same facility that I had faked my way through a decade earlier. The only difference was I now had a probation officer and couldn't just recklessly turn in dirty urine samples. Simple enough—I decided I would just drink more to compensate for having to quit recreational drug use.

Once again, I attended all the classes and managed to flex my work schedule around it. I was drinking before the group met, and I was drinking when the group let out. I was so smart and had it all figured out. I participated in the classes but as a devil's advocate. I would challenge the other addicts and alcoholics. Words like *willpower* and *strength* were haphazardly thrown around. Then, there was an "it" moment.

The leader of the group, Debbie, had already held me after the class adjourned a couple times to confront me about very obviously having alcohol in my system. I would hang my head in shame, refusing to look her in the eyes. She would ask if I wanted to quit drinking. Well of course I did. I just didn't know how. It was embarrassing. I was supposed to be in control. I didn't like imagining life without being high one way or the other.

About twenty of us sat in a big circle for each class. Some were addicted to crack, some purely alcoholics, and some a mixture of everything. It was eerily similar to a shift meeting at work. One day during class Debbie called me out.

"Jamie, I saw in your file you were actually here ten years ago. Is that true?"

"Yes, I was here a while back."

"Why were you here?"

"I had gotten into trouble and moved back into my mom and dad's house. I came here for court. I ended up getting a lot of community service and probation."

"And why are you here now?"

"I got into trouble. I just moved back into my mom and dad's house. I ended up getting a lot of community service and probation. Part of my probation was to come here."

"So, ten years of your life has passed you by and you still sit in the same place?"

I twitched. Shook actually. Very noticeably. I almost fell out of the chair. She had wrapped her fist around my heart and squeezed it. Debbie did a really good job at work that day.

I was awake. I mean finally awake. The truth, although spelled out for me for years in plain sight, suddenly was very apparent. My family had begged me, people had given up on me, and counties and cities were trying hard to make me a permanent citizen in one of their barred resorts. But to wake me up, it took Debbie pointing out that my years had escaped me and I had nothing but shame and lawyer fees to show for it.

For over ten years, I built walls. The biggest wall was built within me, trapping me inside myself screaming to get out.

Build a wall, build a wall, build a wall ... brick by fake damn brick, and then be upset with those outside the wall for *literally being outside the wall.*

Classic. Make them hate you, then hate them for it. Make them hate you, then hate yourself.

"We don't just burn bridges. We go full-blown Chernobyl or Nagasaki on everyone and everything around us."

CHAPTER 9

BURNING BRIDGES

Eventually people will quit asking you to come around and will quit coming around you. Calls and messages will be ignored, traditions forgotten, and familiar faces slowly back away into the crowd. Not just people, but institutions, bars, schools, and places of business, will ask you not to come around anymore. We don't just burn bridges; we go full-blown Chernobyl or Nagasaki on everyone and everything around us.

Part of my story includes a game called "name a state and I'll tell you what I got arrested for." Now obviously I haven't hit the clink in all fifty, but being centered in the Carolinas, I've got a fairly good track record with North and South Carolina, Tennessee, Georgia, and Maryland.

In direct opposition to having those around you who turn away, the legal system opens its arms so ever-lovingly wide. Lawyers, probation and parole officers, and judges— man, they looooove you. They are so happy to make your acquaintance. They love you unconditionally like the big bro you always wanted. All in a sterile, "take your freedom, take your money, and talk down to you" way despite that somewhere deep inside this criminal addict is a decent person who is just lost.

I pause to make it clear I have *zero* resentment for anyone I ever encountered in the legal system. They were doing their jobs. For an industry that would be better off if it could possibly go out of business due to lack of transactions and a clientele population that doesn't want to be clientele, the workers in this field conduct themselves miraculously well. There's a "don't hate the player, hate the game" notion here for those that have continuous run-ins with the law and feel the customer service isn't up to par. A friend that was on his third DUI would vent to me about what an ass his probation officer was. All I could offer was the plain truth that if he doesn't like his DUI probation officers, then perhaps he should stop driving drunk. Again, simple in theory, just not easy to execute.

PEOPLE AND PLACES

Burning bridges at institutions is taking your debauchery to a next level.

Home for fall break from our first semester of college, our usual gang had gotten together and was up to no good. I could say we were unfairly picked on by the police, but I would be lying. Underage drinking, possession of drugs and paraphernalia, and possession of concealed weapons were the charges. We were drinking, smoking weed, and had a couple pairs of brass knuckles. It was well into darkened evening hours. The police had been called when a neighbor saw us walking around the elementary school campus across from my parents' house.

The beer was a no-brainer—we had no business having it since the oldest of us was only nineteen. Shout out to my lifelong best friend to this day for being the one that had the weed in his pocket. It was *my* weed, and the cops found it on him. He took that charge all on his own. Find you a friend like that, but use it for good.

The only laughable part of this delinquency was the finding of two pairs of brass knuckles. I had left my knucks in Baltimore, but my two friends each had theirs, both aptly engraved with "3 Stooges" as we had so eloquently dubbed ourselves when we got them. You would've thought the police had landed a lead on an underground vein of MS-13s or something. Indeed, the knuckles were illegal to possess. They were sold under the guise of a "brass paper weight" at a store where years later I would purchase a sewage-tasting, drug-passing cocktail.

A combination of the three of us, one at a time, would proceed to answer the officers' line of questioning. And I stress one at a time because nothing will bring the "yes sir/no sir" proper etiquette responses out of you like having the police in your face when you're stupidly young and you know you done f-ed up.

Police: "So, the 3 Stooges, huh? Is this a gang?"

Us: "Not a gang, sir, just kind of what we call ourselves."

Police: "How many of you are there?"

Us. "Well, there's three of us. It's the 3 Stooges. You have all of us here."

It was painful, attempting to answer with genuine respect. An encounter with the law has always proven to be sobering, but there was a small giggle when we were being asked how many people were part of the dreaded 3 Stooges gang.

The family of one of the Stooges lived on the other side of a field on the school property. The third lived down the street. This was a level of humiliation that was nightmarish. It was one of many times my father has said to me, "I am not mad, but I am disappointed." These are truly the most painful words I forced him to say to me time and again.

We weren't taken downtown but were given official citations and court dates. The charges all varied, as there were odd combinations of the trespassing, the weapons, who had the alcohol, and who had the drugs. But as an added bonus prize, each charge was compounded with an "on school property" suffix.

It was like the McDouble for our McDumbasses. And with our hands full of citations and paperwork, heads held low as we stood before our parents, we were sentenced on the spot a further decree: "The three of you are to never step foot again on Charlotte Mecklenburg school property unless under direct order of the court." That one stung. We nearly choked as the overpass engulfed in flames.

Not only was I a card-carrying, or brass-knuckle-carrying, member of the worldwide syndicate known as the 3 Stooges, I was also one of the original members of Baltimore's feared Hot Dog Bandits.

In a folly of errors, I was hanging out with some dudes I usually didn't hang with in a place I usually didn't go. A night of club-hopping and debauchery ended with what seemed like an innocent enough stop at a 7-Eleven for a feast of metal-rotary hot dogs.

Here's the deal: I didn't have any money. I can't remember the how or why on this. I simply had no money. The guys I was with assured me they would spot me all night, and so far they had. They were gracious hosts to a night on the town, club cover charges, flowing alcohol, and no complaints. And to be "I just wiped the window with vinegar" clear, I in no way blame these dudes for my involvement. I chose to go out with them. I chose, as someone not old enough to legally drink, to go out with the intention of drinking at bars and clubs. I chose, in complete irrational thought, to go out on a Saturday night … into the city … with not a single dollar in my pocket and zero access to any form of money. These were all *my* choices.

We all rolled into the 24-hour-operating 7-Eleven. As we entered, with no real discussion and no unnecessary explanation, I was told we weren't paying for the hot dogs. Grab them, dress them, and walk out. The guy won't do anything because it's late at night and he won't be looking for trouble. We grabbed the dogs—I actually ate one in the store—and with another in hand and my two friends each carrying two, we simply walked out the door.

The clerk began yelling "Hey, hey stop!" Another important fact is the clerk was moonlighting from his other job as a Baltimore County police officer. So yeah, just letting us walk out wasn't his mindset. We had barely gotten our feet out of the store onto the concrete jungle when blue lights were *everywhere*.

I froze. They ran. I was brought back into the store and given the chance to pay for my hot dogs and be set free.

I. Had. No. Money.

Cuffs it was, and I was thrown in a squad car. After a few minutes, my fellow larcenists were dragged to the car. There were a couple bloody lips and eyebrows, some rips and dirt all over their clothes. Evidently running led to a bit harsher reaction from the police. I'm not sure if they were offered the same "pay and go free" option I was, but judging by their apparent physical treatment I'd say that was a hard pass.

We rode in together, all three in the same car, but somewhere along processing we got separated. I wasn't issued any county blues, but I did have my belt and shoestrings taken from me. I was given a cot in a small holding cell, slept a few hours, and went before a magistrate of sorts early Sunday morning.

This two-dollar hot dog now ballooned to three hundred dollars in court charges and fees. The judge, bailiff, and all the officers I encountered through this whole deal thought it was hilarious that I was being arrested and processed as a criminal for stealing hot dogs. We were dubbed the Hot Dog Bandits, and I was asked, "Did you at least put chili on them?" and other humiliating questions. It was definitely a low, yet not quite ready to bottom out.

As the magistrate rattled off the necessities of paying my debt to society, which included the financial offerings and an ungodly amount of community service, I was also instructed, by the standards of the private business being represented, to never again set foot in any 7-Eleven anywhere in the United States.

These might be laughable at best, but how about multiple arson charges?

PLAYING WITH FIRE

One night wandering the halls of Goucher College, I simply couldn't find anything better to do with my time. I was living in the dorms, had no roommate, and my usual cohorts all had things that they'd rather do. Hanging with me at this point wasn't a special occasion; in fact, this was a weekday and just outside of finals. People were studying, going to bed, and living normal, responsible college lives. And I was on a continued downward spiral.

Most of the campus was asleep at this hour, but I was drunkenly stumbling about with no destination. I ran into a couple buddies that were on their way to their rooms. They looked like they had indulged, but they knew when to call it a night. I intercepted them and told them to come with me. I led them to the "quiet hall," a coed-by-floor dorm that had strict quiet hours. Noise pretty much was a no-no from 10:00 p.m. to 10:00 a.m. daily. It was a haven for students that were super serious about their studies and quiet time. Some really cool people lived among these halls, just with no excessive raucous activities. You know, normal people.

So, I figured I'd just set the mf'er on fire.

I can't honestly say that was a well-thought-through plan. I took my two buddies into one of the communal bathrooms, and I lit several rolls of toilet paper on fire. They saw no humor in this, cautioned me to stop, and ran off. I ran too, but not before lighting several more things on fire along the hallway toward the exit—even the door decorations of a good friend of mine.

Being a small campus, I was back in my room before I even heard the inevitable alarms. I passed out in my own sweat of criminal stupidity before all the dorms were evacuated and people were being accounted for by authorities. I was in my familiar, warm, drunken comatose state as Baltimore County police organized safety huddles in the parking lot and the fire department made sure all the emergency sprinklers had effectively done their jobs. I caused and missed all this scary, life-threatening chaos.

The next day the student body rose and went to their classes. I slept late as if I had nothing to do. My class attendance was almost nonexistent by that time. I hadn't completed any end-of-year projects and was going to fail every final I took. I saw some of my closer friends later that day, and although it was never said to my face, I'm pretty sure they knew.

I walked among my fellow students, acting clueless about this event. People were mad. People were scared. Some people got caught up in possible theories. The Baltimore County boys in blue were all over the campus as was the Baltimore sector of the FBI. This wasn't a joke anymore.

I once again did what I always had done: I hid. I stayed in my room, self-medicated, and just pretended to not be there. I was taken into the security office by the police and questioned once. I gave a recount of my day and night of the fire, with my story ending conveniently right before I ran into my two friends. I knew this wasn't going to just go away.

The next day, I awoke to the sound of multiple heavy footsteps with a few jinglejangles of stainless steel. This was it. A knock sounded at the door, and two uniformed police officers accompanied by Goucher's head of security were standing outside my room. A simple "come with us" was offered, and to their credit they spared me a little humiliation by not cuffing me right there and having me walk to the security office shackled.

At the security office, it was explained that I was being arrested for multiple counts of arson plus handfuls of other charges. I was going to jail because I potentially could've killed a few hundred people in their sleep who had done nothing to me, had done nothing wrong to anyone, and were just sleeping in a trusted place as they chose to further their education. I was the biggest asshole this small community had ever seen. And as I was loaded into the back of the squad car, I was told to never step foot on any property of Goucher College ever again.

As the car pulled away, I looked over my shoulder through the back window. I was watching my college career engulfed in literal and metaphorical flames.

The last person I saw leaving the campus was exiting one of the buildings, most likely on her way to class. It was my friend whose door I set on fire.

"Nonaddicts, nonalcoholics, and 'the regulars' can't imagine how we 'choose' to live the way we do."

CHAPTER 10

COMPLACENCY LOVES COMPANY

Complacency is just as much a killer of spirit and drive as drugs. We don't get sober to waste our life. Comfort is a killer. It is easy for an addict/alcoholic to thrive in misery even when sober. No longer doing drugs and drinking alcohol is undoubtedly the most important part of sobriety, but it doesn't end there.

Spiritual clarity is what is needed. Complacency is not what you need.

Spiritual clarity isn't sitting on an isolated mountaintop humming your days away. Spiritual clarity is being aware of what your heart wants—what you desire and what motivates you. It's embracing the realities needed to achieve. Rest. Diet. Education. You keep your business clean. Clean your yard. Leave things and people better than you found them. Don't just dream. Plan. Manifest. Put in the damn work. Be honest with yourself and kind to yourself.

We need to live sustainable lives. We need to take care of ourselves and those that depend on us. We need to be loving humans. But we don't need to wallow in our own sewage pretending it's what we want. This is what we do as addicts. Live in a daze. Lie to family. Sacrifice our job and education.

LIVING THE LIE

We befriend those whose only interests are being as much of a loser as we are, with the only common denominator being everyone else has turned you and them away. So hey, bottoms up! We're pirates! We're outlaws! They just can't handle us! Lies, lies, lies. It ain't just a Guns N' Roses album. It's the constant dishonest validity we give ourselves. We will legitimize that we are okay because we still have a few friends. Through acts of addiction and lack of accountability, these are what we refer to as Lowest Common Denominator friends.

Complacency shackles the addict. Nonaddicts, nonalcoholics, and "the regulars" can't imagine how we "choose" to live the way we do. The answers, the solutions, are indeed very obvious, yet they're just not desirably attainable in our minds.

First, we have family. I feel deep sympathy for anyone that loses their family's support and love. Sometimes it's not even our actions but things like money, political views, chosen lifestyles, and partners that can tear families apart at their very foundation. Throw in the insufferable addict and we're not exactly Miss American Pie.

I am fortunate. I never lost my family. I wore them thin. I pushed them to the utmost limits. But they never gave up on me. I am not worthy of such a blessing. I am one of the lucky ones.

After family, you have friends. This starts socially at school and expands with clubs, sports, and similar interest groups, then continues into the workforce as we grow. We enjoy engaging in activities that interest us.

LOWEST COMMON DENOMINATOR

As we allow our obsessions to overcome us, as we explore the world with our distorted sense of ourselves, and as we become less and less tolerable through our habits, we begin to lose friends.

Our family is weary of our presence. The study group doesn't want you around because you show up wasted. The ball team doesn't want you at games anymore because you passed out at second base. Your work friends don't tell you where the meetup is after work anymore because you take a two-drink postshift cocktail hour and turn it into a blacked-out cocaine-fueled time warp lasting three days.

You become uninvited. You are outcast. You are no longer a joy to be around. The interests that attracted you to so many people of similar leisure are now second to living as an addict. Addiction comes first and you try to fit the rest of the world around the schedule of using and boozing. There's just not enough time in the day.

We lose our ambition, we lose our interests, we lose our friends, and at times we lose our minds.

Like a lost asteroid haplessly floating through space, eventually you will crash into another space rock. One that has also so unjustly been cast away from his or her family. One that used to be so active but now all their friends have turned their backs on them. Stronger than any polarized magnet, nothing attracts more quickly than one beat-up, living-in-denial loser to another beat-up, living-in-denial loser.

To be clear, this Lowest Common Denominator friend, or sometimes friends, can be a buddy situation or an intimate relationship. And at the core base of this friendship is an underlying truth: there isn't a damn thing in common among them all besides the fact they enjoy getting f-ed up and no one else cares to be around them.

I saw a buddy go through this firsthand. I went through it myself, but being sober and eyewitnessing this rang loud and true.

Kaiser was a respectable dude. I met him at a place we both were working. I was his boss, and he was eager to help out and a hard worker. He was joyful to be around and very reliable.

And then things started changing. To be specific, a large ingestion of pills all day, every day began to happen.

A slow slide into being unreliable led to evictions and waking up with mystery bruises and cuts. Being broke. Severe weight loss. Lack of hygiene. It was an avalanche of watching someone crumble before your eyes.

The rest of the staff began distancing themselves, no longer welcoming him to the group. An island to himself, and he really thought no one noticed.

Then, a new friend started popping up. Someone that would pick him up from work, hang out at the bar waiting for Kaiser to get off, and disappear into the night with him. The guy was well known in the area and wasn't known for anything good.

I could see this happening and still allowed Kaiser employment. He would show up, clumsily bulldoze through his shifts, and be out of my sight before any major catastrophes. When he was done with work, he and his new friend—the LCD, as we will call him—weren't allowed to hang out on the premises. Who knows where they went? Many times they didn't know themselves.

TAKING A BULLET

I gave Kaiser a ride home one night as LCD had somehow secured a job and was getting off later. He explained to me how great LCD was and how the two of them were just misunderstood. You know, it isn't the square peg's fault the hole is round.

Then Kaiser shook me with a comment I had heard countless times before, but I swear I can't recall hearing it since then. Maybe this was its exit from my conscious.

"LCD would take a bullet for me."

Dafuq?

Kaiser got out of my car and that statement just resonated with me. "He would take a bullet for me."

I thought, I don't want a friend like that. Sure, I want a true friend of integrity and loyalty, but I don't want to be in a situation where bullets are coming at me. I don't want to put a friend into a situation where they are taking bullets. I don't want anything to do with any bullets.

I don't want someone relying on me to take a bullet for them either. No way, no how. Like, bro, sorry but you're gonna die. That's your bullet. We shouldn't even be here.

Family? That is different, and I say that speaking specifically for the three others who share the same roof as me. Without hesitation. I know undoubtedly those kids would be raised pristinely by their mom, and I will absolutely not have one of my children removed physically from this earth before me. So yeah, *that* bullet? Sign me up.

But I continued to think and realized the truth in my own existence.

My best friend took a bullet for me with my weed in his pocket. Bang.

My family took several bullets with lawyers, late-night calls, and endless worry. Bang. Bang.

My friends and coworkers had been riddled over and over again with a machine-gun fury of lies, deceit, betrayal, and selfish decisions. Unaccountability, physical violence, destruction of property ... Bang. Bang. Bang.

I realized I don't want anyone I care about taking a bullet *for* me just as much as I don't want anyone taking a bullet *from* me.

The guns that shot all these bullets are long gone. The chamber's empty, unloaded, and properly stored. No one will ever take a bullet for or from me again.

Once you enter this mindset, it is a strong circle where there is no room or need for complacency. Only when your bullets are replaced with awareness, hope, and clarity can recovery finally begin.

"I was nurtured by the fruits of this hypocrisy as an employee. I then turned right around as a manager and fed my employees the same blind-eye entrée."

CHAPTER 11

LOOKING THE OTHER WAY

Employee/employer enabling for the addict is just as present and deniably destructive as the blind eye you receive from friends and family. If you can show up relatively on time, not set the place on fire, and fulfill your job directives with minimal damage, then your employment is zip-tied, super-glued, and duct-taped securely in place.

I'm not speaking as if it is a restaurant-industry-specific problem, but I can tell you we food slingers live and work together as a highly diverse group. It's an industry that welcomes all ages, from late-teen front-door greeters to full-time laborers in their seventies and beyond. Think of any paradoxical spectrum and it is present in this crazy community. Teachers and students. Parents and children. Lazy, "white collar take it for granted" silver spooners and the appreciative "I fought for my life fleeing Cambodia as my family was assassinated" folks. Loners. Those waiting on their "real job," whether to finish school, move up in management, or have the random porn director come in and ask if they'd like to be cast. These aren't jokes. These were my coworkers.

And you also have my type. I started as an "I have nothing else to do-er." Being competitive in the worse ways possible, I was quick to realize there are three ways to get respect in this industry. You outwork everyone. You out-party everyone. Or you are the most batshit crazy mother trucka in the room. I was determined to be all three.

WORK HARD, PLAY HARDER

For me, and the industry I was in, it was crippling for my addiction. Anyone who has spent a couple of paycheck periods in the food-service industry, specifically restaurants, knows that this environment is just short of being a rock star. There's the sex, there's the drugs, and if you count late-night drunken karaoke at the staff's favorite watering hole, there's even the rock and roll.

We work together, we argue, and we fight. We slip off to our cars in the parking lot, catch a high, and slip back in. We congregate among barstools. The same two who an hour earlier were sailor-mouthing each other about not brewing enough coffee are linked arm in arm for party central.

This behavior might be once a week or once a month for some. It might be daily for others. Hell, it might be twice a day for those working doubles. For some it never affects their job. Some might have a later-than-planned night, show up five minutes late after calling in to let the manager know they are a little behind, and come in and sweat it off. Swearing to never be tardy and work hungover again, they stay true to their self-promise.

Then there are the heavy hitters. They either can't control or don't wish to control their partying. There's no concern with scheduling their entrepreneurial pharmacy deals in agreement with their work schedule. Some slide into the building for their shift on time, in uniform, and completely schnockered. Servers and cooks alike have made many Visine executives reach their bonuses. Plus there's always the excuse of "I just woke up," "I just took a shower," "I got something in my eye," or my personal favorite, "I just got something in my eye when I woke up in the shower." Stumbling might be obvious, paired with the ever-popular perfume of burnt halitosis and booze mixed with undertones of opium—the aroma of your drunken, hungover, stoned, geeked-out cooks and servers.

What happens here? Does a member of the staff get sent home? Does the establishment wish to operate shorthanded? There are a lot of variables. Is the impaired employee capable of performing at a level with minimal damage that will outweigh the damage done if the servers or the cooks are short one? Does the manager want to set a precedent of discipline due to intoxication? This could wipe out a large majority of the staff. And what if the employee in question is one of the better employees? We see it in pro sports and in entertainment—athletes and actors that have serious attitude, legal, or substance abuse problems who are quasi-contributing employees due to their work performance. It happens in the less-glamorous restaurant world time and time again. Unless the employee is unable to stand on their own accord, if they show up, they are more than likely going to be allowed to work.

I was nurtured by the fruits of this hypocrisy as an employee. I then turned right around as a manager and fed my employees the same blind-eye entrée.

Kaiser would show up on time, get his station set up, and then take a break. He'd go outside to smoke a cig and return to his position. Then for an hour he'd be fighting passing out. Every day. Eyes would roll back, he'd stumble forward, he'd drop the spatula to be startled by the sound of it clanking on the ground. But he kept on working. And he was, before and after the coma-like state following his smoke break, a pleasure to be around. Polite, funny, and most importantly a hard worker.

Obviously, there was something more than nicotine being ingested during this smoke break, but I chose to ignore it for the positives he provided. There are no "bench players" in the kitchen. You don't have a staff sitting around waiting to sub out. You don't have extra cooks on the clock waiting around. Profit–loss businesses have to operate with minimized expenses, and that means running with the fewest people possible in the kitchen. If one of them seems to be on heroin or a handful of pills, look the other way if they are "sort of" doing their job.

FORGIVE AND OVERLOOK

Often our loved ones can be crippling roadblocks to our recovery. Our family and closest of friends want what is best for us, but they also don't want to see us in pain or need. They don't want to see us suffer, so they loan money. They provide support, shelter even. They ignore warning signs and destructive behavior. They keep picking us up when they need to let us fall and stay down until we are ready to get up on our own.

I was a disruptive asshead in school, starting from middle school on. I thought I was hilarious. I now realize I was ungodly obnoxious and often impinged on other people's experience. But I was young and for the most part a good student. It was easy to forgive and overlook.

In college, I violated a lot of the dormitory rules. I was openly underage drinking, smoking weed indoors, vandalizing, and harassing students. But I always went through the forgiveness motions and initially was a good student athlete. It was easy to forgive and overlook until it wasn't.

As a manager in a restaurant, I put partying ahead of my job performance. Name a rule, and I broke it—from employee fraternization to being full black-out drunk during my shift. But I deemed myself a company man, and I knew all the right things to say and when to say them. When it really counted, my performance would stand the test, so for the most part while on the clock I was viewed as a good employee and supervisor. It was easy to forgive and overlook until it wasn't.

Believe me. Sometimes the worst thing a family, friend, coworker, or manager can do for an addict is forgive and overlook.

❝ With a united persona of pushing
way past any respectable limits,
the drinking to excess was getting
worse and worse during shifts. **❞**

CHAPTER 12

MANY LAST CHANCES

Early in my career, not every day involved ingesting microdots and blotters. I had a taste for the daily highs. We had a blast chiller in the walk-in cooler. A blast chiller is designed to bring prepped items down to a proper temperature below the temperature danger zone for storage in the cooler. It was basically a large closet—a rectangular room with an intense cooling fan blowing. It was also a perfect hidden corridor for smoking weed.

Luckily for me, we had baked potatoes on the menu and were always needing fresh chives cut. Per protocol, cut some chives, lay them on a sheet pan to cool down, and take them into the blast chiller. As quickly as possible, take out a prepacked bowl or one-hitter, light it up, and blow it into the fans. Shake the pan so the fresh onion smell covers up any residual reefer orders. Revisit the chiller a couple times to shake the chives again just to allow their odor to permeate. I tell you the God's honest truth that we *never* ran out of chives at this place.

Any nose candy or pills could be ingested with more discretion. It wasn't necessary to cover up any odor with prepping menu items. It was also advantageous to become friends with the bartender. Any drink rang up errantly, sent back by the guests, or made by mistake would find its way back to my workstation in a standard to-go Styrofoam cup with lid and straw. If we wanted to have more drinks than the charity was allowing, we could just start our own bar tab.

A server has a section of three, four, five tables. Everything that is rang in by that server is coded to one of those tables. A bartender has a whole bar. Granted, there are bar stools, but sometimes there are people standing and mingling. A guest might come up to the bar from his table where he's dining with the family and need to sneak a bourbon real quick. There's a glitch in the system where a bartender can have an uncountable amount of tabs open at any given time. If there is a tab opened to "Bob" and it just happens to be me and three cooks racking up drinks while we're working, no one really notices.

EVERYTHING IN EXCESS

With a united persona of pushing way past any respectable limits, the drinking to excess was getting worse and worse during shifts. Staff members were disappearing to take prolonged smoke breaks. We were starting fights with each other. And then the ultimate faux pas: we started to f-up the food. Burning stuff, wasting food, allowing ticket times to get too long ... we were starting to blow it. And as much as the servers and bar staff thought we were cool and loved hanging out with us, they did not play kumbaya when their income was threatened. Animosity and resentments were starting to set in.

A star server named Jones had moved up to a management position. Promoting from within is beneficial in any industry. In a restaurant, it's a huge benefit because a lot of the basic knowledge is already learned. Starting out as an hourly, nonauthoritative employee, you have a lot of friends. Once a manager, those friendships are frowned upon. I wasn't playing by these rules. And upon his promotion, neither did Jones.

The downside of Jones's promotion was he was one of a few that I allowed my work performance to slip around, and he wasn't happy with me. Neither was his circle of friends. As I continued to show my ass at work stumblingly raging through shifts, Jones would stand back and take it all in. He was also forming a formidable friendship with the general manager, so it was only a matter of time for the inevitable.

The termination went down quickly after a trilogy of just completely stupid acts on my part. After a shift full of enjoying cutting chives and storing them in the blast chiller, I was on my way out for the day. The GM stopped me to have a relevant work conversation, and I unknowingly had my ridiculously large bag of weed sticking out of my front pants pocket. He stopped midsentence, plucked it from my pocket, and shook his head in disgust. He pushed me away with the hand holding the bag of contraband and let it drop to the floor. Whatever he was debriefing me on became lost, and he walked away shaking his head in disappointment. I thought for sure that was going to do it.

Unscathed and unlearned, a few days later I was still acting stupid, carefree, and untouchable. I had just scored a bag of high-grade grass from a coworker. At this point I honestly hadn't even smoked any. Impatient to get home, I pulled out the bag, unrolled it, packed a one-hitter, and deeply inhaled a few whiffs of its glorious aroma. I walked past the server station and the odor was so pungent that everyone caught wind of it and quickly looked in my direction. There were a few "good god" and "what the hell" comments. It had a smell so strong it was as if I had lit an entire bush on fire. To make it worse, the servers were gathered in their station being instructed by Jones. I thought for sure that was going to do it.

Since I didn't get fired *again*, it took me a whole day to let my guard down and continue my idiotic behavior. I was running a closing shift and had quite a hefty bar tab, mostly from some blue-colored concoction. The closing manager was someone I got along with well. As we shut the place down and all the employees left, the front-of-the-house manager finished up all the daily tallies and I sat at the bar. For about an hour in solitude, I helped myself to draft beer and smoked weed as if I were relaxing at a hostel in Amsterdam. Eventually the manager finished up, we hung out for a bit, and then headed out. All normal enough, right?

That happened to be a Friday. The next morning at nine o'clock there was a staff meeting for all employees: managers, servers, bussers, host staff, back of the house ... everybody. As people came in and found their cliques to sit with, it was the usual staff meeting parade. There were those that went to bed maybe just two hours ago and a few that got way overprepared and overdressed for this function. People came in sweats and baggies, and a few that had to open after the meeting came in their work uniforms. But everyone was there.

These meetings have a usual agenda. This meeting started differently than any other.

WRITING'S ON THE WALL

The GM, standing on an elevated level splitting two sections of the dining room, started off. "I will pay anyone ... ANYONE ... a substantial reward for any information on whose the eff *THIS* IS!" Held in his hand was my bowl that I had left, packed with weed, on the bar the night before.

F-ck.

Being that the GM knew which kitchen manager and service manager closed the previous night, I was certain he had the owner of the smoking piece narrowed down to one of two people. On top of that, I remember looking around the meeting and counting to myself the number of people who knew that the pipe was mine. Easily over half, maybe even three-quarters of the staff had smoked from it as I passed it to them. Work friends are one thing, unsolicited monetary rewards are another.

No one said anything and the meeting proceeded normally from there. I thought for sure that was going to do it.

I worked that day and was clinched so tightly I could whistle Dixie out of my ass. The next day, Sunday, came and I was just as stressed. There were constant talks of the pipe, and every time I looked up Jones was staring at me. I used classic, shameless kissing-up antics on the GM—following him around, laughing at his jokes loudly, praising his intellect, and seeking his favor. This day, too, came and went. Maybe I was in the clear?

Monday came and let's just say I never saw Tuesday. As I entered the back door for my closing shift, one of the other kitchen managers stopped me with "Fields is here man. They've redone the schedule and you're not on it." Fields was the area supervisor. For him to be there unannounced meant something was going down. I considered just walking back out the back door and leaving, but thought maybe, just maybe, I could get away with a warning of sorts.

I walked in the office where Fields was waiting on me. He had a manilla folder on the desk in front of him with my name on it. He opened it as I closed the door behind me, and there were several documentations of "incidents" I wasn't even aware were an issue.

He went through this file and there were multiple signed complaints from employees about my drugging and drinking while on the clock. There was the "weed in the pocket" ordeal. There was the "made a section of the restaurant smell like Jamaica" fiasco. And it all concluded with the "got so high you left your stash behind on the bar" night from three days ago. I had nothing to stand on, literally bracing myself on the door behind me.

I signed a series of papers and was told I could quite possibly be rehired if I were to receive some sort of counseling. I left in tears of shame, as I was throwing away a very good job that offered many great benefits. Mind you, I got into restaurant work because I couldn't get my life together, now I was spiraling even more out of control because I couldn't get my life together. Actually, it was more like diving headfirst and oiled up down a metal slide.

I did what any self-respecting alcoholic and addict would do—I went and got f'n ripped. Three week bender. Loaded from sunup to blackout. I was mad. Mad at Jones. Mad at the GM. Mad at Fields. Mad at the entire staff. It was all their fault. Everyone was to blame. Everyone but me.

"The only person who can decide when we are ready for change is the same person killing us. Ourselves."

CHAPTER 13

EVERYONE'S BOTTOM IS DIFFERENT

You hear about the "bottom." For the addict that is fortunate enough to work on themselves and turn their lives around, it all starts at the bottom. Their bottom. *The* event. *The* final devastation. The pit of hell. The final powder-laced straw that breaks the back of the camel, the drug mule, the elephant in the room, and every other damn animal on Noah's Ark that he had to build to survive the flood of your bullshit. But not all bottoms are the same.

I found myself playing cards with my homeboys at a house on the south or west side of Charlotte. I'm not sure whose place it was, but the four of us dudes were mirrored with an equal number of females.

Per usual, I was trashed. Blitzed. Fully loaded and only interested in furthering my buzz. Nothing else really mattered. A couple of the dudes were flirting with our counterparts, while Master P rapped the classic "How Ya Do Dat" in the background. I was sailor-on-leave drunk, but I'll be damned if I didn't notice one lady across the room was missing a leg.

I stood off from the card table, steadily drinking and smoking. As a few games of Tonk played, the driver of our group had been sliding closer and closer to Miss Eileen, the lady with one leg and the tenant of the house. I figured that out because I'm a detective and noticed the amount of prosthetic leg pieces in the bathroom.

After what didn't seem like a long time, my three dudes made it apparent we were leaving. We shuffled out, saying goodbye like I was departing my best friend's house.

In the car, I had to know a few things.

Me: "So, she only had one leg ... that lady back there?"

Them: "Yeah man, her old man shot her leg off ... blasted her with a shotgun when he found out she was cheating on him."

Me: "Oh damn! I guess he's locked up?"

Them: "Nah, they're still together. He was on his way home actually, that's why we had to bounce."

Again, I was as drunk as an Irishman on Saint Patrick's Day, but I heard that loud and clear.

We were just hanging with someone whose lover blasted her with a sawed-off shotgun. We were just casually chilling, easy like Sunday morning, with someone whose husband knowingly tried to kill her.

Not just that, had he not given a courtesy call on the way home, we too could've, best case of a worst-case scenario, spent the rest of our lives buying our shoes at half price.

That was not my bottom.

INCARCERATED

I was sitting in a sector of the Baltimore County Detention Center, facing multiple arson charges and having no clue of when I would be getting out. A fellow prisoner, one of the tier leaders, slid me a rubber-band-bound package and told me to hold on to it. No questions asked, I held it for a trip to the infirmary, held it for a shower (don't ask), held it while watching TV, and went to sleep with it. He knocked on my cell door sometime during the night and asked me to open it up and slide it under the door.

Now I couldn't just open my cell door and give it to him because it was locked, as his should've been. Yet there he was. Silly prison.

I took off the rubber band, unrolled the envelope, and my heart stopped. I had been carrying around two cigarette lighters for about five hours. I was being held for arson charges and I'm walking around this joint with literal fire in my pocket. Holy. Effin'. Ess.

Still not my bottom.

Dad: "So, where are you watching the Tyson–Holyfield fight tonight?"

Me: "Chub is picking me up and we're going to go hang with his family in Fort Mill."

Dad: "Just be careful."

Me: "Of course, Dad."

The next day, news articles and coverage on the local channels reported the "minor riots" in Fort Mill where a few were injured and two cop cars were vandalized and damaged.

Still not my bottom.

DUI with the front half of my car gone. Multiple arrests everywhere I went. Negative bank account. Crossing lines I swore I would never even approach. Fights, self-abuse, failing health, life-threatening event after life-threatening event.

Not my bottom. Not my bottom. Not my bottom.

Another thing to understand is reaching one's bottom does not mean being all alone. People can bottom out all by themselves in an extended-stay hotel room they can't afford just as easily as they can bottom out in their very own all-brick mansion surrounded by family. This can happen while in the midst of being a social butterfly with *real* friends and it can occur drifting with the tide with a few other scoundrels. The disease of addiction does not discriminate. That is a clear truth. Also true is when the alignment of *all* of you—when your spirit has had enough, your heart is ready for change, and your brain has even the slightest glimmering, brief shining moment of realizing a change is needed—when *that* universe comes together, that is when you decide you have gone down far enough. Your bank account doesn't matter. The company, if any, you keep doesn't matter. Employment status, relationship issues, your ranking in any hierarchy you participate in ... irrelevant. Bottoms are as fingerprint-unique as snowflakes.

DIFFERENT BOTTOMS

I knew of a guy that reeked of cheap, dime-store aftershave. Not because he was fond of too many dabs behind the ears, but because he drank it. His alcohol tolerance had grown so high and so many corner stores had cut him off as a liability that he *had* to drink aftershave. And he still hadn't hit his bottom.

I can tell you of someone who has since become my friend but at one point had a substantial amount of body parts detached from their core. Through modern medicine miracles, all the king's horsemen and all the king's men put this Humpty back together again, and yet he was buying crack on his way home from the hospital. Not his bottom.

I witnessed a friend become unemployable due to an incredible cocaine habit. Declared bankruptcy and maxed out no less than a dozen credit cards. Guzzled a bottle of vodka right in front of me before insisting I drive them to a 24-hour, county-run detox joint. We were denied access because the level of intoxication was too high. Too intoxicated for the county to be held accountable. Too intoxicated for detox. Not the bottom quite yet.

My cousin had the world at his fingertips, man. Great looking dude. Crazy talented musician. Even had the megacool oversized dog. Made a *splash* of an impression on a certain blonde Hollywood leading lady. And he couldn't keep it together. No matter the success, all the dreams coming true, living a life envied by all—he constantly chose the drink over all the good in his life. He didn't see it as a bottom. In fact, he never lived to see his bottom.

A very, very good friend of mine was charged with a hit and run, with kids in the car, and also injured a pedestrian. Some contraband was found at the time of arrest (this person did go back to the scene, in their defense). They spent exuberant court costs and a week in jail. Admitted to smoking broom bristles while in the clink. Not the bottom.

I can spare the details of day-in-and-day-out pain, but two friends from years ago ran a parallel path. DUI. Again. Again. Again. Time served. DUI again. Suspended license. DUI again. License permanently revoked. More DUIs. And neither of these guys ever even got the chance to reach their bottom.

Sadly, I know too many people who didn't have the fortune of recognizing they had bottomed out. Or recognized it but didn't make the decision to change.

You reach bottom. You recognize bottom. Or you die. No job can save you. No family. No education, wealth, or social circle. The only person who can decide when we are ready for change is the same person killing us. Ourselves.

The severity of bottoms is unique. The emotional turmoil, the financial costs, the pain felt and caused all vary from one to another. But when it finally hits, brother let me tell you— it *hits*. Hard.

One of the biggest obstacles we put in front of ourselves is admitting we are wrong. Opening up, realizing we need help, and being willing to pursue it is the biggest admission for us. It is, in a sense, the bottom of our bottom. But it is also our turning point. It is where we have marched to the gates of hell, dragging many that we love with us at times, gotten as close as we can without being engulfed, and realized it is time. This is wrong. I am wrong.

There has got to be a better way. I am ready to find that way. I am willing to change. And from the most wretched time of our life, we begin a journey to the spiritual promised land. Pack accordingly. It wasn't an overnight trip to the bottom; it's gonna be quite a hike to get out of this mess.

There are endless nightmares, both my own personal and ones shared with me. But only the addict can decide when enough is enough. And sometimes, for the dedicated and fortunate, that enough leads to recovery.

REACHING BOTTOM

Finally, for me, it was sitting in a holding cell waiting to see a judge. The small cell was designed to comfortably hold a single prisoner, but I sat in there with twelve other orange-jumpsuit-wearing fellows. And in a room so small you could sit on the bench that ran along one wall and reach your arm out and touch the opposite wall, a grown-ass man almost pissed in my face.

At this point I realized I had to make some changes in my life.

It's an incredible range of feelings when a conscious bottom is reached. *The* bottom. The one that makes you truly say *enough*. There's obviously some sadness. This is what I have done, and this is what I have caused. The dreams, the young kid that knew no evil, the aspiring success story ... wasted, literally by many definitions, day in and day out.

There is fear. Fear of change. No matter the level of depravity and despair our daily life has become, it is oddly comforting. It's scary to leave that comfortable hell, knowingly afraid that we are going to have to feel. The masks are removed, and the lies are no more. We want out of this hole and it requires truth and changing our ways. Terrifying.

There's hope. We think that maybe, just maybe—the smallest maybe of all maybes—we can turn our lives around. Maybe we can get moving in the direction we feel we were supposed to go all along. We still just might have a chance. No one gets sober without even the faintest glimmer of that hope.

UNWRAPPING ADDICTION

As someone who manages addiction and has witnessed others battling addiction's noose, I know your reality is what you decide it will be.

"I'll call my addiction Stuart if I want. Arguing about what addiction really is, that's just another smoke screen."

CHAPTER 14

WHAT IS IT REALLY?

Addiction is absolute soul corruption. It has nothing to do with intelligence, morals, willpower, or common sense. Addiction is a very slow, tedious suicide of your soul.

People have passionate arguments about what exactly "addiction" is. Is it a weakness? A disease? A state of mind? A mental illness? "Who cares?" is always my answer. Who freaking cares! I'll call my addiction Stuart if I want. Arguing about what addiction really is, that's just another smoke screen.

Addiction is the most laborious decision of giving up. It requires so much work. Scoring, indulging, and recovering. Lying, hiding, and manipulating. Rationalizing, justifying, and validifying. It requires so much effort. Working so hard to do the wrong thing. Death would almost be an easier option, both for the addict and any family and friends that are still present in their lives. The sadness of death is without a doubt an extreme low, but it is a final answer.

Despite having the world at his fingertips, despite being the life of every party and everyone's best friend, despite being the classic "all men wish they were him, and all women want to be with him" guy who seemed to have an unbridled love affair with life, Craig, that mentor and hero to me, decided he didn't want to live anymore.

Whether an overdose, a suicide, a murder, a car wreck—even a freak accident—the circumstances may never clearly give an answer, but you at least know it is over. The worry, the concern, the impending feeling of doom is all gone. But an active addict is forever on the dope clock, and their loved ones are constantly in an emotional-limbo hell.

The screen an addict will throw between themselves and the work needed to work on themselves is intense. If you're an active addict, you shouldn't worry how addiction is categorized; you should focus on getting clean. If you're an addict in recovery, you shouldn't argue with others; you should embrace the way you found recovery and help others that are interested in following a similar path.

If you are not an addict of any kind, then it is absolutely none of your business to put a label on it. It is a weakness. It is a disease. It is a state of mind. It is a mental illness. It is a spiritual malady. It is a hole in your soul. It is a lack of strength. It needs a cure. It is an absence of mind. It is an overpresence of mind. It is all of the above. It is none of the above. It is the exact answer to all the questions it asks.

YOU DECIDE

We find our recovery using the same methods and tools that got us in trouble to begin with. We are the only ones that can diagnosis ourselves. An addict is an addict when they decide to admit to it. Not when they are told they are. And an addict will recover when they are ready to recover. Not a second sooner.

Addiction is unmanageability. An addict cannot manage their life. An addict can manage and "control" other things, just not the one most precious thing we all have: the job of keeping our spirit, mind, and body healthy. I could manage my bills, I could manage my time, I could manage my hobbies and interests, but I could not manage living with an active addiction. I could even hold jobs where the word "manage" or "manager" was part of the job title, but I could not stop myself from making knowingly piss-poor decisions.

I have to drive. Get drunk anyway.

I have to be up early in the morning. Do the cocaine anyway.

I haven't been to this class in weeks. It's okay. Eat the mushrooms.

You're only young once, right? Ignore long-term plans and seek immediate gratification. You know what you need to do. You just can't manage to make yourself do it.

Addiction involves living in a world of false reality. The only perspective we concern ourselves with is ours. We control the thoughts of others and base our actions and reactions on the thoughts and motives we forcefully instill upon them.

There is a heightened focus on "us," on our importance as individuals. We are center stage, the starring role. All those around us are merely extras for us to use at our own discretion. With some, we might form closer bonds. Others, we use only for the benefits we can leach off them. For many in our lives, their existence is obsolete if not in our presence. We force upon them our perceived thoughts, our perceived emotions, and our perceived reactions. We form their script into what is needed to fit the sequence. We are all controlling and completely driven by our ego.

Guess what happens when people don't follow the script. We flip the ever-loving bejesus out, that's what.

JUST A SYMPTOM

The ailments of addiction span beyond the drug and alcohol abuse. There's more to it than that. There's the spiritual malady, the feelings of inadequacy, the fear of impending doom, the imbalance of being on top of the world mixed with despair. The drug abuse is just one symptom.

Addiction will enter your mind and soul and hang up one of those tacky Halloween decorations boasting "abandon all hope ye who enter." What starts as a party every now and then when the timing is permissible slides into parties when the timing isn't so permissible. Then more and more frequently. From "hey I got an extra thirty minutes to spare, let me catch a fix" to "I'll just not do this thing that I should be doing for the sake of the fix." From a fun little side thing to the thing that everything else revolves around.

The ingestion of drugs isn't the core problem.

The core problem is the uneasiness we experience with ourselves. That unbearable uneasiness is the spiritual ailment—the hole we need to fill, and the chase for which we never obtain. We're in a full-blown sprint with no idea where the finish line is. The use of our drugs of choice is how we deal with it. The using and boozing is a side effect, a symptom.

For whatever reason, we are restless, irritable, and discontent. There's worry of uncertainty. There's obsession with what we can't control. There's a bloody white-knuckle clutch on to pains and mistakes of the past. So we drink. So we drug.

The real work is to journey inward. To see where we began the journey of this train of thought. Why we commit to this painful existence and torturous mindset every single day. To see *why* we resent. *Why* we hold on. *Why* we fear, obsess, destroy, and avoid. But until we are ready for that spiritual awakening, it is easier to just get lost. To make our reality what we want it to be. To lie to ourselves and say we are comfortable in a compromised life.

Being an addict or alcoholic doesn't mean you are a daily user. It doesn't mean you wake up in the gutter with a brown bag in hand and eat out of trash cans. Not all alcoholics and addicts live in abandoned train cars and wash windshields at red lights.

DEPENDENCY VS. FREQUENCY

There are plenty of alcoholics and addicts that use or get drunk once a week. But when they do it's an obsession. It's an obsession for days heading into it and regrets for days coming thereafter. There's a loss of control once the events are underway. I mean *big* loss. "Normals" may have done those one or two little oopsie nights. I did a decade or so of oopsies. But this goes beyond the one time at summer camp or the office Christmas party. It's an unveiling of a Jekyll and Hyde persona that you don't just wish the world wouldn't see, but you also wish it didn't live within you. The drugs help. They are an easy solution.

There are plenty of complete full-blown addicts that wake up with no snooze at 6:35 a.m., do a few rounds of calisthenics, and kiss their wife and kids goodbye before heading into the office. This is done Monday through Friday, and the weekends are spent alternating between golf courses and horse races. The cars are nice. The kids are smart and the bank account stays healthy. But it's the closeted, hidden drinking no one knows about. It's the uppers midmorning and the downers after dinner. It's the desperate feeling that the days wouldn't be possible without these. It's the fact that these forms of self-medication are being used to compensate for the inadequacies felt at work, the sorrow of seeing the kids grow up, and the insatiable fear of bankruptcy despite the bankroll. In fact, this exampled fella *knows* he has so much money he will never go bankrupt. But if he can make himself worry about that, then that fat line of cocaine he's doing in the parking lot of his office building while contemplating going to work or swallowing a slug out of his loaded Glock is justified. It's how we think, it's what we do.

You don't have to have lost it all. You can, in fact, be still functioning and be a successful student, athlete, and/or businessman or woman. The boats, the car, the good grades, the gold medals ... these don't make you "okay" and they don't make you infallible.

Losing it all doesn't include physical property. It doesn't include money or job titles. Losing it all is when you can't recognize yourself. When your soul left you long ago and you can't remember the last time you were genuinely happy. When every day is a burden to just exist. When the world feels against you. When you push everyone away and let no one in. When the lies move from your loved ones to yourself.

That's when you've lost it all.

You will know when it happens.

Knowing it has happened is pointless unless you do something about it. As my experience goes, you do not take that spiritual journey alone. Living the way you wanted to live and not taking care of yourself is what got you to this bottomless pit of darkness. You sure aren't crawling out of it on your own.

Addiction is 100% nondiscriminatory. Skin color, race, religion or lack thereof, economic background, education—none of that matters. It is the mindset. It is the hole that needs to be filled. It is the overcompensating of mind-altering substances to cope with having to look at the self. Self-image. Personality quirks. Social inadequacies. Character flaws. I don't care what side of town you drove from, the condition of the car that got you there, the job you clocked out of before arriving, the family you might have or might not have given a "see you later" to before leaving the house/apartment/tent, when you enter an AA or NA meeting, the insides are all the same. The core existence is the same. It's daunting.

RECOVERING ADDICT

Being an addict in recovery unlocks mental and spiritual freedom that not everyone attains. But sometimes we never get past the exterior of some of our best potential teachers. Living life the way we always have, viewing the world the way we always have, making decisions the way we always have— this is how we got here. To think we will crawl out of our holes, get our spiritual locomotive back on track, and have any kind of enlightenment if we continue *our* way is just foolish.

We must seek help. And not just from those that favor what we believe *looks* successful. We must see past personalities and beyond outer appearance. Our soul is broken and suffering. We must listen to other souls and hear the essence of other people, regardless of any outer shell.

You will find those truly qualified to help you have endured this journey themselves. The time for judgment on our side is long gone. Humility begins with listening and hearing.

The question of "what is addiction" might be definitively unanswerable. The understanding of recovery is just as elusive. Abandon all reasoning ye who enter. Throw away all schools of thought. Disregard all past methods of rationalization.

The road to recovery, the journey, the mindset needed to travel this successfully will require an entire cleansing and reprogramming of your psyche, attitude, and outlook. For it has been the corruption of these parts of us that got us here in the first place.

**❝ When you are in denial,
reality isn't what you want.
Escaping it is. ❞**

CHAPTER 15

LIVING IN DENIAL

Mind-melting tripping experiences always ended with the whole coming down—the coming back into reality. I cannot emphasize enough how much I hated it. On a trip, I was everything and everything was what I wanted it to be. Time was irrelevant, everything was fun, and everyone loved me.

When I could feel the turning of the final corner toward the inevitable downer, I would become depressed. The ride was drawing to an end. This isn't an endless disco. There are responsibilities. The real world is still here. The world, that for whatever reason I hated but in return honestly treated me so good, was still here. And I didn't want to come back to it—reality, that is. When you are in denial, reality isn't what you want. Escaping it is.

Things started to get out of hand for me in high school. Denial was setting in.

I was concerned about driving under the influence. I was worried about getting into the house under my parents' radar. I also had (misdirected) blind faith that I would be okay. Well, instead of a blind faith, it was more like a hard squint.

I believed—because it fit the story I was trying to create in my undeveloped brain—that the persona I wanted to appear as was comforting the scared, real me with sweet caressing reassurance. I can still be in control. I won't get hurt. Nobody will get hurt.

Just a reminder, no one really was in as much awe as I thought they should be. So, I pressed on.

GETTING WHAT'S DESERVED

We complain about not getting what we deserve. I know I haven't gotten all I deserved, and I'm quite fortunate for that. I deserved way more than one DUI. I deserved to be locked up for several drug trafficking, distribution, and using violations. I deserved to be locked up for arson. I deserved to be dead from several accidents where somehow I just landed correctly. I deserved to be cast away for putting my family and friends through so much. Lying, cheating, stealing. I deserved so much more pain and punishment than I ever received.

Denial can happen, especially when you are first attempting recovery. As I entered my first stint of AA at twenty years old, I saw this fifty-year-old, toothless Black lady and told myself, "Nah, that ain't me."

I saw the arthritically crippled old man telling horror stories of driving his car backwards through the rain since the transmission was blown and he was determined to score crack rock, and I would say, "Yeah, I'm better than that."

All lies. All self-hate and falsely elevating my sense of worth. As I scoff internally at these people who are way worse than me, it never really crossed my mind that they probably never set fire to a building that housed a few hundred college kids just trying to get a good night's sleep.

The stories, the details, the exterior that you can see simply function as wrapping paper to fool you into believing you don't belong in recovery. You aren't *that* bad. You look at the exterior. You see your opposites.

The present is on the inside. The recovery is learning about others so we can learn about ourselves. The recovery is unlocking a self-awareness that not everyone is privy to or ready to embrace.

My very worst day could have easily been someone else's best ever. For that I am grateful.

LOWERING OUR STANDARDS

We deny because we never get "that bad." We never stoop to lows that we set as standards. When we do, we lower the standards. We blame the world around us—the people, the rules, the weather, anything and everything. We hold ourselves accountable for nothing and project even our conscious wrongdoings on others. We become so engrossed that we feel like we're pulling it off, even though the lies and life we try to tell and live are so insultingly obvious to those around us. To let go of that denial, to acknowledge our faults, to embrace truths allows our spirit to expand. The truth is easier to carry. The right thing requires less cleanup. Honesty isn't hard to remember.

One of the biggest links on the shackles of addiction is denial. Even at times we know we're lying to ourselves we continue to lie. This is the belligerence. This is the cloud we live in, the fake world we created. So deep in denial we descend that it is hard to even fathom how much easier life is when we accept the world, we accept those around us, and we accept who we really, really are.

❝Nothing in life is free. You aren't owed something for nothing. Period. But life can be rich and that is the irony.❞

CHAPTER 16

NOTHING IS FREE

Here's the secret to a happy life that I fought long and hard to discover.

Throw in a dramatic scene of a snowy tundra, with me fighting against the elements to reach the pinnacle. Atop the highest mountain sits the guru messiah of all tranquility, and it is from this Zen master that I learned this truth.

Get ready. Grab a highlighter. Snap a picture or at least fold the top corner of this page.

I bestow upon thee the secret to an eternity of bliss: come to terms with the fact that the world doesn't owe you a damn thing.

And there you have it.

For people who suffer with addiction and for all people who have a hard time finding their seat at the table of life, once this secret is accepted we can feel the current stop pushing against us, and it finally can get behind us and help push us along.

There isn't a "fair." People that work far less than you will exceed way further than you. You will see the same person win at bingo, the lottery, the dunking booth at the pineapple festival, and the free-car giveaway at the new all-you-can-eat joint across the street from the renovated Starbucks, all while you stand there and question, "Why not me?"

You've exhausted efforts, stretched funds, studied long and studied wrong, and brought yourself physical and emotional pain through stress-fueled preparations, all to fall short. Again and again.

I once studied myself into a migraine in high school. I had to go to the ER because we didn't know what was going on, and I refused a spinal tap to test for meningitis because I had heard that was a way LSD could be detected. You get that? I would rather risk a viral death then have my father sitting beside me find out I had taken hallucinogenic drugs.

The world is not going to give you what you want. I have found it to be true that with proper preparation, proper effort, and no lie, absolutely some good fortune, the world will give you what you need.

This isn't about how many people you can talk off a cliff or how many thousands you can donate to selected charities. Treating the world around you better doesn't involve grandiose acts. You look at the grandest structures, both of nature and man-made. Walls, trees, buildings, pyramids, and waterfalls are massive but started with that one single nail, seed, brick, or opening. That one single drop of water. One root that reached even deeper. Then it becomes something more, and it grows and grows.

HARDER LOOKS EASIER

It's all about shopping carts and turn signals, man. Really, it can be that simple.

Put your empty cart in the cart return area. Use your signals when turning and changing lanes. Even when pulling into your driveway. Even when no one is around.

The true character of a person, their inherent absolute worth, can be determined by how they act when no one else is watching. Put the cart back. Use your signals.

The shopping cart returning is both a literal and metaphorical situation. Literally, because for countless reasons, if you don't return your cart, you're an asshole. But I think many of us have witnessed people working way harder to hoist their empty cart on a curve, or walk further to put it with the stray flock of other unloved carts. We will put forth more effort to do something wrong. We will go out of our way to do, intentionally, what is not expected to be normal. We know we are doing wrong, being an inconvenience to others, thinking that simple rules don't apply to us, and then we wonder why the world is so unfair.

I don't care what you believe—be it God, a higher power, or none of the above. I don't care if you're into the retrograde of Mercury or trying to find out ole Jim Jones's Kool-Aid recipe. I can tell you this with unequivocable certainty: The world is a living, breathing, all-knowing, and powerful force. It knows. I swear to you on a stack of whatever you want to stack up. It knows.

You will be amazed with how the quality of your life improves when you start playing by the most simple of rules. Start with putting your shopping cart up. If you don't believe me, do it for a year. No excuses. One year of determined, pristine shopping-cart discipline. If your life hasn't at least leveled out, much less improved by leaps and bounds, then get in touch with me. I'm accessible. I will refund your misery. No questions asked.

Nothing in life is free. You aren't owed something for nothing. Period. But life can be rich and that is the irony. Once you embrace that nothing is free, you can live freely.

The constant pursuit of a deal is gone. The cost of dishonesty, the half efforts, the backtracking, and the cover-ups are all gone. These spiritual maladies cost more than anything we will ever purchase and they run with an interest rate higher than me on a Tuesday afternoon. This isn't just a financial charge. Those are easy; they don't hurt our insides. It's all the shortcuts, low blows, and easy way outs. The "no one is looking, no one will know" moments where we sacrifice just a little bit of our integrity to take more than we should. These choices are what have the highest costs. These acts destroy your moral compass. These acts drive a wedge into the ease of committing more heinous acts more and more regularly. It's one thing for something to cost you money. It's another when it shackles your soul.

A handout from a friend isn't even free. What does this cost you? It costs you the act of returning the generosity when you can. Not all costs are bad, you see. Much like a profit-driven economy, the more "costs" we all have circulating that provides positive energy to those around us, the more all of us will thrive.

Eliminate the pains that destroy you, that enable others, that take away from joy. Leave the world, the people, everything better than you found it. Oh, you were fortunate enough to have your coffee paid for by a stranger? Well, it really isn't free. You now have a debt to the world for providing more positive energy. It isn't a cost, but an investment into our wholeness. Our happiness. Our charity. Our purpose to be good rather than corrupt and self-serving.

❝ Being afraid of having to give up their evils, vices, and shortcomings before they can be accepted is what is the problem in the first place. **❞**

CHAPTER 17

WANTING RECOVERY

I started culinary school during full-blown alcoholism. Seldom sleeping more than three hours a night, I would drink a beer on the way to school to get me going. I would drink during school. I would drink on breaks. This time frame coincided with the brief life span of a certain 8% alcohol energy drink on the market. What a time to be an addict. I would drink after school to get ready for work. I'd drink all through work and go to the point of blackouts after work. Wake and repeat.

I finished culinary school with a year of sobriety and a newfound self-respect. I had run full tilt on cheap gas for so long, it was amazing what could be done with proper rest, self-respect, and a more appropriate view of my position in the universe. I was able to communicate more effectively with others. I was able to focus on my job, and I was able to be accountable and uphold commitments. Above all, I developed faith. True faith. Not hoping that all will be okay, but knowing everything is going to be alright.

I can't paint a complete rose-colored image. I stumbled, and still do. Frustrations, ego-driven decisions, and lapses in judgment still happen. But daily, sometimes even hourly, a spiritual inventory is done to make sure I am not going astray.

Stop, slow down. Why are you doing this? Why are you having these thoughts or feelings?

Evaluate. Honestly tell yourself when you are wrong. If needed, seek counsel of people who you know will be honest. I am talking authentically honest. I don't understand the phrase "brutally honest." It's either honest or it's not. There's no "brutally friendly" or "brutally kind" or "brutally humble." Don't seek advice from those that will give you the answer you are looking for. Seek advice from those that will give you the answer you need.

SOBRIETY'S IRONY

The method I chose to explore to achieve sobriety required a completely backward way of thinking. All through life, whenever experiencing something new or taking on a new task, you receive information first and then are expected to learn and perform. A new job will put you through training before allowing you to work fully independently. For a sport, you will learn basic fundamentals and have practices before you have an exhibition or game.

When learning to drive, how insane would it be for a driver's ed teacher to throw you behind the steering wheel on the interstate with no knowledge of street signs, which pedal does what, and how to drive with your knees while you roll a joint? Okay, the last part might be for a later class.

Now let's venture into the world of AA and the insanity that Alcoholics Anonymous uses for recovery. When you join, there's no training, no explaining, no dual steering wheel joined with a tetanus-infused bicycle chain. You just dive in and hope there's water in the pool. Deep down inside, you know that metaphoric water is there as you meet and see many people within AA swimming right along. Some are graceful as swans. Some are bobbing and fighting for their lives. Some you might see get out, leave, and come back again later—hopefully. You hope this water will keep you afloat as well. But one thing is for certain—you'd better jump your ass in and paddle, swim, or whatever it takes.

You show up to meetings. You make coffee. You don't know why, but someone told you to make coffee. You get strangers' phone numbers. Lots of phone numbers. You call them even when you have nothing to say. You help people you don't know. You listen. You give people rides. You see people that have a sobriety, a life, a peace of mind that you think you might want to achieve, and you are instructed to flock to them.

You are also not to judge. Some of the best people I met at AA were ones who I would naturally propel away from for superficial reasons. They were missing a tooth. Their shoes were dirty. Their car was beat up. I would look for the slightest reason to be offended and then rationalize to myself for hating them. For years and years, I had built up this horrible, conceited wall and never allowed myself to see people's true worth. Their value. Their soul. To be honestly active in AA, you must tear down that wall. Or you die.

CHOOSING RECOVERY

There are plenty of external factors, no doubt. We choose to live clean, to be sober, to wish to achieve because of our family. For the promise of a promotion. To save up for that once-in-a-lifetime trip. But only if *you want to* will it be made possible. You can be pushed, prodded, intervened, guilt-tripped, court ordered, and maybe stumble into a meeting just looking for shelter. But until that light goes off in your head and your heart that recovery is something you need, something you want for your very own well-being, then it can be considered a lost cause.

You can fake your way through a job. You can live unfaithfully in relationships. You can play the game on cheat mode, and you can even at times put your trash in your neighbor's receptacle. But you can't cheat recovery. Take it from me. I tried, and I know many others that have as well.

You have to be driven. You have to *want*. Where does that drive come from? What awakens the beast of need inside us? Many things, many different things for many different people. But once it's awakened, you will know. I often have told people: If you are not fully committed to recovering and changing your life, then don't even bother. Go have some more fun and/or misery. But do come and see me. I will be here. My story and advice will remain the same.

Recovery is all about action first. Just dive in. Follow direction. Perform tasks. Help others. How does collecting five phone numbers a day keep me sober? Don't worry about, just do it. Take the action. The recovery is happening without you realizing it. As you are learning to tread water in the waves of a tsunami, you will be helping others swim without realizing it. This is how it works.

At first, people want to hide and don't want to commit. Being afraid of having to give up their evils, vices, and shortcomings before they can be accepted is the problem in the first place. As it was explained to me, bring all your evils to the party. Bring all of who you are. Your higher power already knows this about you. Fear not but walk with faith. You show up and the cleansing will occur. This is how it works.

We work with the faith that we will be paid at the end of two weeks. We flip on a light switch with the faith a bulb will illuminate. We fall thousands of times a day with the faith our extended leg will catch us with the next step and we march on. With faith alone we walk. If we can do it with all these simple things, truly we can do it with the spiritual well-being of our lives.

I came to a crossroads. For years and years, I pushed these thoughts away. Thoughts that I'm more than this and that there is more to life. Thoughts that I have a grander purpose not just for myself, but for those around me.

TAKING INVENTORY OF SELF

What I have realized is that it is dangerous to compare yourself to others; but, at first, I looked immediately to my family.

My father had helped set up the infrastructure of Mecklenburg County and keep it stably running. His father, in fact, was the first Mecklenburg County Manager. My mother took seasonal, charitable jobs. This team of Mom and Dad is forever present, engaged, and aware.

My oldest sister is a definite rock. She's not only raising her two boys but dedicating her life to education. She has more degrees than I have arrests at this point. Her career went from teacher assistant to teacher to vice principal to principal to regional superintendent to something that I don't even know what the title is. She lives in Charlotte, has an office at the University of Virginia, and works in the Southwest United States helping underdeveloped, underfunded schools. When she speaks people listen, as she is a trailblazer in her field.

My other sister is the most free-spirited of us. She is a dedicated public servant, working in many social service settings and elementary schools. I always admired her ability to follow her heart. For a while she shuffled job descriptions to follow her children through their school paths. Now she has dedicated her life to being in the best physical and psychological health possible and encouraging those willing to join her on that journey. Her husband, like our father, is present at baseball and soccer games and still excelling through the ranks of the police department to become Lead Homicide Investigator.

And here I am. The young one—the one that was going to conquer Hollywood, conquer sports, become a big name. I was going to own the world. The genius, the nerd, the athlete, the overachiever. Here I am. Flipping f'n burgers.

ONE STEP AT A TIME

When in AA, it is suggested that you don't change too many things at once. I didn't change career paths in my first year of recovery. But I fell to what I would classify as lazy, convenient living. I took sure shots, taking a route and positions that I knew were pretty much guaranteed to keep me comfortable. I made money. I made a family. I'd like to think I created a stable, mostly healthy and positive work environment.

Despite what appeared to be getting into a more stable routine, my soul was hurt. I wasn't the man I wanted to be for my family. I wasn't the roaring success I wanted to be. The money I was making compared to my time invested wasn't balanced. It didn't make sense anymore. I wanted to live fearlessly. I wanted to live freely. I wanted to challenge myself and others. It came time to change.

At the age of twenty-nine, on September 29, 2005, I finally decided to no longer be defined by my addiction and -isms and that I had had enough of the misery caused by alcoholism and drug abuse. In that last year, my normal daily intake was forty beers paired with smoking weed all day long while being willing to put mostly anything anyone would offer me into my body. I was lucky to only have one DUI. I was lucky to not be incarcerated. I was lucky to not be dead.

It is when your soul starts to hurt that you know you must change.

Recovery isn't the end. It can naturally be dreaded even though active addiction was dredged in flour, hit with an egg wash, and double breaded before completely golden frying our brains and spirit. The miserable existence we created for ourselves is helpless yet at the same time comforting because it is what we know. We have built a steel fortress of deceit, cowardice, and corruption. We look at the changes needed for sobriety to be just as helpless and the road it leads us to just as dark.

Nothing could be further from the truth.

Lots of addicts in recovery speak of the intangibles, of the unseeable gifts we are given with our new lives: self-love, appreciation for the now, serenity, a new lease on life with new priorities.

These are fantastic. These are the reasons we choose to change our lives. But let's be honest here. We are trying to live. Like *live*, live! There is a fear that with this great spiritual change we will be robbed of joy. Numb to pleasure. That life will be pointless and less fun without inebriation.

That's the evils of addiction talking to you. Tell them to shut up. This isn't exactly a Dr. Seuss book; I hope I'm transparent with that. But, boy, the places you'll go!

WITHOUT SHACKLES

Initially, I was scared. Scared to leave the house. Scared to feel any extreme emotion. Scared to experience life.

When you are ready, you will know, as will those around you. That's why we don't tackle this beast alone. We have our support groups, our circle, our sponsor, and sponsor family. Reach out and ask. If you're ready, they will let you know.

When we embark into the world, it can then be without shackles. There's no trepidation, for we have been allowed to walk among the world and to do so with a sober mind. No drunken stagger. No ulterior motives. Not looking to score, to cheat, or to rob. Not having to lie or pretend. We enter society honestly, and it is more of a kaleidoscope of people and feelings than we remembered.

I remember going to the mall for the first time sober in probably ten years. Sometime back I had gotten a green-and-black-paneled ball cap and I wanted a shirt to match it. I went to the mall. Talked to the employees at the store. Engaged in banter. I didn't tilt and wasn't asked to leave. I said things, people responded. They said things, I responded. We laughed, we flipped our hair, we batted our eyes. I found the shirt. I bought some shoes as well, and even purchased a pair of old-school jumbo laces for s's and g's.

I wonder at times where that one came from—s's and g's ... shits and giggles ... that must've been a hell of a party.

But back to the mall. It was liberating. It was a simple pleasure I had taken from myself—not allowing myself to function properly because I had to be stoned and drunk and whatever else to make it to the mall. My funds were previously limited, as I was also holding out for alcohol and drug purchases. I'd have to stop at a bar of some sort in the food court or nearby, then drunk drive my way home or to the next joint for more using and abusing.

It was a special day, that day at the mall. Simplistically special. I still have the shirt and the shoes. The laces are still around also, just on a different pair of kicks now.

And when I come across these things I smile. It's another personal victory.

"It's not easy to make the changes. It's easier to sit in the giant pillows of bullshit you have made so comfortably for yourself."

CHAPTER 18

SIMPLE, NOT EASY

It would be pretty lame if the highlight of my recovery story so far was a pair of all-black Pumas and a crispy green Hurley shirt. It wasn't these possessions but the act. The reward. The assurance from the universe that it was still there and I was welcome to join it. Or in this case, rejoin it.

Guess what. I was welcomed back.

Did you know you can go to professional sporting events *and not drink*? Or hypothetically speaking, not do blow off the back of the handicapped toilet? And oddly enough, Budweiser was still sponsoring the Charlotte Hornets and Miller Lite was sponsoring the Carolina Panthers, and subtracting my financial contributions from these sponsors didn't put anyone out of business. Didn't they know how important I was?

You can go on a cruise and not drink. While those around you need life preservers as they drown themselves in Costa Rican rum, you can sit peacefully without temptation, share laughs, sing along to perennial crowd favorites "Livin' on a Prayer" and "Cupid Shuffle," and enjoy the moment. No blackouts. No ship prison. Living, not just existing.

The biggest excuse I would tell myself about sobering up was nothing would be fun. What a lie. Not only are things enjoyed on a secular level, there is no trouble involved! You don't hate yourself in the morning, and you don't owe anyone apologies. It is amazing!

Something you hear all the time in recovery is "it's simple, it isn't easy". It's not easy to make the changes. It's not easy to clean yourself up, to work on your shortcomings, to attempt to mend troubled relationships, to try to get back on the progressive educational or professional track.

It's easier to sit in the giant pillows of bullshit you have made so comfortably for yourself. Listen to how ridiculous this is: it is easier to wake up (if you are lucky enough to have gone to sleep) and your first thought be, "I have to get high." It has gotten easy to find the fix, to try to appear to function normally with whatever daily duties you might have— school, family, job. At this point, even recreational activities are a burden because they take away from the high time.

It's easier to ditch friends, lie to parents, and fail classes. It's easier to get fired. It's easier to put yourself and others in danger by driving when you can't walk. It's easier to shut the world off and to sit alone in your dark hole. It's easier to ignore your pain and turn to drugs and alcohol. It's easier because the drugs and alcohol are the unique things that fool you into believing everything is okay. The job has demands, the school has tests, the family has expectations— the drugs and alcohol, however, have the lie you want to hear.

The solution is simple. Put the drink down. Put the dope down. It just isn't easy to do when your brain, no longer on alcohol or drugs, isn't telling you what you want to hear.

VULNERABILITY SETS IN

What happens when the addict, when the -oholic, decides to get clean? What happens when the unthinkable sobriety is achieved? Now we are vulnerable. Now we must feel. It is easy to hold ourselves back, to not live unrestrained out of fear.

It's up to each one of us as individuals to show up for ourselves every day. Every day. Yes, there are bad days. There are don't-get-out-of-bed days and going-through-the-motions days, and those days are necessary. We must reset. We must refocus and rest. And at times we must hide.

But each of us, every single one of us, is ultimately responsible for our own fight. And we must be there for it. Subjectively speaking of course, you can call it your fight, your journey, your battle, or your story. Hell, just like addiction you can call it whatever you want.

Notice the beauty of how anything and everything around you is defined based on how _you_ want it defined. Regardless of the description, we are all here and we all must make the most out of it. _You_ can fight your fight. These positive relationships along the way will most definitely assist you at times, but it is important to remember that people are looking to win their battles or enjoy the journey or ice their cake or whatever metaphor you have for being the best you can be.

I don't care who you are—your gender, race, economic vitality, or age—your daily responsibilities are simple. One, wake up. You can't be part of this world while sleeping. Two, take care of yourself. This is ongoing all day. Eat. Clean. Earn. Help. Pray if that's your thing. Rest. Observe. Teach. Do these things to keep yourself healthy and functional. Three, you must take care of those around you. From houseplants to children to elderly parents, we all have beings, entities, and even possessions that rely on us and need us. Without taking care of ourselves first, we are useless to those people and things depending on us.

Now naturally, as humans, we complicate this. Everything needs money. Things need time invested. There are just and unjust hierarchies all over the place that we can choose to be part of, choose to distance ourselves from, or attempt to overthrow. We can settle for a job or pursue a career. Pursue a purpose.

Standing up for ourselves is necessary at times. Knowing when to wait patiently is equally necessary. Every yin and yang, every polar opposite is present in our daily lives, and *we* must be the ones to represent ourselves in these days. To put our best foot forward. To know what we want, how to get there, and to put that into action.

No one will fight your fight.

No one will run your journey for you.

SLOW AND STEADY

It's suggested early in recovery to not make any drastic changes in your life: don't change career paths, don't abandon (or start for that matter) any new relationships, don't make life-altering or potentially life-changing decisions. The decision to start to live sober is going to rock your world hard enough. (Yes, after over a year of sobriety I asked my sponsor if it would be cool to pursue this super-hot firecracker I had met at work.)

When I started to get sober, I had been in the food-service industry for close to ten years. So I did what I was told: stay the course, continue the necessary curriculum, go to AA meetings, work my shifts, explore the 12 Steps, work with others in recovery, work alongside others neck-deep in the decadence of party town.

I was very protective of my restaurant work. But for *me*, for my experience, it wasn't a good match. Being a slave to substance, a prisoner to complacency, made it an industry where I could find the abuse I love.

This is why recovery is simple, not easy. Because addiction shows up as an element of surprise and reality long after you stop using and drinking. You just choose something else to be your addiction. Or maybe it chooses you.

" It took a long time for me
to realize I had been living
the addict life for a long,
long time. **"**

CHAPTER 19

REPLACING, NOT FACING

It was suggested to me while getting sober that we must be wary of substituting something in place of our drug, or drugs, of choice. Some people begin to experiment with drugs they've never used before, reasoning that the old drugs were the problem. Some people may start using relationships as their new crutch—both intimate and casually social acquaintances. They indulge in the thrill of newfound friendships and in going through the ritualistic getting-to-know-one-another dances. Making connections, making plans, and then becoming obsessed with exploring the newness until eventually they self-sabotage the friendship in pursuit of another. Once that puppy smell goes away, it ain't so cute anymore.

As it was explained to me and understood by me, my state of addiction didn't lie solely in the use of drugs and alcohol. It was the pursuit. The distraction. The hole filling. The hiding. The chasing. The inflated feeling of self-importance. The rush. The thrill. The anticipation of the next round. And the next round. And the next round. And again. And again.

I did the shoe thing. The hat thing. The T-shirt thing. Collecting collections. Careful to honestly be aware of my motives. Is it for *me?* Is this something I really want and will enjoy, or is it for the nonexistent game of cool that no one else is really playing?

But it was fun. I enjoyed the toys I grabbed. I would talk myself off these ledges and back to reality, justifying each action.

DRUG-FREE, STILL AN ADDICT

It took a long time for me to realize I had been living the addict life for years. After giving up the dope, after shaking off the withdrawals and sweats, after having the obsession of the crave for a high being removed from my body—I was still living the life of an addict.

I played by the rules. I stayed at the same job. I finished my school and pursued no kind of dating relationships. But the career I had chosen was another comfortable hell. As I learned who I was, as time marched on, as I became we and we became family, I quit growing. I replaced. I knew it. And I was scared—scared of what I had become and scared at the prospect of having to change. Although I didn't like where I was, it was comfortable. There were no surprises. The worst thing for an addict is change, but change was needed. Real change, not just a replacement to fill a gap.

That's when the ultimate addiction became clear. I was addicted to my restaurant life. It was a replacement, not an escape.

I was years and years both into my sobriety and into my career before realizing this. I mean *realizing* this. Feeling it.

Burning bush, cloud splitting, clap of thunder, booming voice of realization. I had traded in the drinking. I had traded in the getting high. I had traded it for the same experience that I had created for myself, which made it justifiable in my thinking.

I put my career in front of my family. I would constantly try to outdo anyone around me, even at the expense of my own general health.

"Oh, you can go fifteen hours? I can go seventeen."

"Five hours of sleep? What is that, two nights' worth?"

"Fourteen days in a row? I'll do twenty-eight."

The most satisfaction I would receive was from the often-bestowed-upon-me "I don't see how you do it." I'd smile like it was nothing. Do the "gotta do whatcha gotta do" John Wayne mosey off into the sunset. But I did it with an unhealthy amount of sleep deprivation. I did it with an unhealthy amount of caffeine. I did it by ignoring my knees, my ankles, and my back telling me to take a break. I did it by turning my back on my friends and family. I did it by making my love be a single mom from Thursday to Monday. I did it by never seeing my family on the holidays. But damn, I did it. And it impressed people.

I transitioned from dealers and bartenders to my boss. No workload was too much. No task was insurmountable. There was nothing I was afraid of. Pour me a shot of "we're going to be really busy" and I'd down it like chilled Jager. Again and again. As others fell off, I stayed. Shut those bars down. Day in and day out.

"What about your family?" I'm here, it's what I do.

"Aren't you tired?" I just keep going.

It was this rush, this pursuit, and this perception of

overcoming challenges that kept me high. I couldn't get enough. I could feel it rush through my veins. I would turn evil if challenged. I treated people very badly if they stood in the way of my success—in the way of my high. It's what I had control over.

As an addict you realize you can't control the world, but you can control what you are putting into your body to help cope with your feelings. As a sober addict, an alcoholic in recovery, you still can't control the world, but it's best you find ways to deal with it. To look reality in the face and accept and recognize what you are doing to yourself, again. The lies you are telling yourself may be different, but they are lies all the same.

I don't have to be a father. I don't have to be contributing to society. I don't have to go to my friends' funerals, weddings, or cookouts because I am at work and *that* is what makes me feel good. I don't need your reality. I don't need to feel. I don't need to grow. I put away the straw and was out of the bar, but I continued to keep myself high with the rush I got from my job. Let the world burn in hell for all I care.

SWITCHING IT UP

Be wary of the replacement phenomenon. A lot of people fall victim to the obvious, indulging in a different intoxicant. From hard liquor to beer. From alcohol to weed. From cocaine to hallucinogens. In the head of an addict, it makes sense. Like, come on my man, you're not even trying. You ain't even sober. Surprisingly enough, many try to rationalize this.

There's also materialistic replacement. The shoes. The big toys like boats and bikes. Even with these, the pursuit is often more exciting than the actual ownership.

My shoe collection, for example. The anticipation is fun. Trying to score some limited editions or shoes that for some reason have personal nostalgia is another rush. But once attained, they often get thrown into the used pile of toys as the next pursuit is being planned.

I've had to talk myself off many ledges with these purchases. An honest, sincere inventory of myself: Jamie, you don't need these. You can use this money in a much more responsible fashion for your family. You only want these to impress this pretend fan club you have. To be "better" than someone who is either not aware of this popularity contest or, even worse, who doesn't even exist.

The shoes weren't killing me, though. The shoes weren't taking away from my soul.

So, where's our happy ending? Our happy ending lies in the fact that we are addicts. We are relentless. Tirelessly aggressive. Not just driven but unstoppable. We attacked our addictions daily with the most goal-oriented drive a human spirit could muster. Despite lack of money, physical and geographical obstacles, or any inconvenience, we would find a way.

In sobriety, we must channel that ruthless aggression into a positive direction. We had an existence largely centered around obtaining and achieving. As villainous as our addict life was, the same powers can turn us into a hero.

We. Are. Unstoppable.

Pursue purpose. Obtain growth. Achieve everything you have ever dreamed of before becoming drawn and quartered to your own indulgences.

An addict is savage. An addict in recovery is un-damn-deniable. Same weapons, same skill set. The aim has just changed.

❝The story of recovery continues here. Getting rid of the booze, getting rid of the mind and mood altering substances is not the end all.❞

CHAPTER 20

ACCEPTING THE WHY

Acceptance. Acceptance is huge. It's also one of the dirty words, one of the make-your-lips-sneer words. It's key, and it's a major key to self-awareness, but it's painful. Acceptance is truth, and truth is what active addiction and alcoholism robs us of. To accept means we must face the world as it is, not as we hope it to be.

There are definite limitations. You don't "accept" a situation that puts your life in danger. But you do accept there are countless things, people, principles, pets, places, and even other words that don't start with *p* that you have absolutely no control over. No influence over. No power. Nothing. And you must accept it.

As much as I try to express myself originally, sometimes repetition of the comfortable truth is the only way to say something.

If you look up "insanity" in an archaic book of reference or using the newest google machine, many definitions are offered. They are all what we have deemed as insanity, all

something we can read and nod and say, "yeah, that's it."
But a paraphrased definition of this word for those that
suffer with addiction, and irrational thoughts all together,
is "repeating the same behavior over and over again and
expecting different results."

This time it will be different. This time it will be different.
This time it will be different. It never is.

Way before drinking, when I knew little of the world's
evils and thought everyone died of old age, I was already
a slave to this definition of insanity. The most poignant
memory I have of this is the bunk beds.

OBSESSION'S INSANITY

I was around ten years old when my parents got me
this sweet set of bunk beds. Unlike the traditional barrack
style, one directly above the other getup, these featured the
bottom bunk on wheels. Made to stick out perpendicular
from the top bunk like an *L*, it also came with a dresser that
fit snuggly under the top bunk. With the bottom bunk on
wheels, you could switch it around to your liking, with the
dresser on the left and the bottom bunk L-ing out from the
right, or the bottom bunk coming at you from the left and
the dresser on the right. It was pretty cool.

Somewhere, somehow, I ran across an ad for a similar-
styled bunk bed set. This one included in the pictures how
the bottom bunk could be turned parallel and slid under the
top bunk à la more traditional style. Now this was exciting.
I couldn't wait to throw this option into my prepubescent
interior design regimen.

To spare the drama, it didn't fit. I remember moving a
whole bunch of stuff out of the way in my room full of "I

want, I want" and having to pull the accompanying dresser out far enough to swing the bottom bunk around. When I lined up the bottom bunk to slide under the top, it simply didn't fit. The overdone craftsmanship and hardware of the bottom bunk made it about an inch too long. This dream of having an interchangeable normal and L bunk set was shattered. Or was it?

Your resident hero here figured maybe it was just too long the way I chose to slide it under. If I reversed the north and south poles or if I were to spin the bottom bunk in a 180, maybe then it would fit. Because you know, if the average ten-year-old boy is five feet tall from head to toe, he loses two inches if you measure from toe to head. This was the logic I hoped to employ.

I pulled it out, gave it the old spinarooni, and guess what. It didn't fit. I'd like to note that it was also around ten years old that I started incorporating cuss words into my daily, normal vocabulary.

Begrudgingly, I reset the beds back the only way they were meant to be—the L now mocking me as the loser I was for not having the super cool, Swiss Army knife of bunk beds. I'd like to say this was the end of this story. Sadly, it isn't.

Over the span of the next five or so years, I tried at least three times a year to see if the L could be transformed into the parallel. I guess it goes without saying that it never fit. Nor did it ever fit when I would give it the spin around and swap ends. Never. This was a glimmer of true insight into what would be a few decades of insane behavior and an aversion to acceptance.

As addicts we choose not to accept things. It gives us reason to fight. We invest our spiritual ammunition into battles we really don't believe in for the sake of the fight itself. The more we fight, the more anger we have or the more sadness we have. We choose not to accept. We choose not to pursue the happiness of acceptance. We choose to make ourselves miserable because *that* is a reason to use. It is a horrible, self-woven, perverse circle of existence. I destroy myself to provide reason to destroy myself.

CONSUMED BY CONTROL

Right when I decided it was time to get sober, I bought a new refrigerator. Buying major appliances isn't one of the 12 Steps. I needed it because I was doing the whole "starting over" thing and had moved into my own place. Kinda my own place.

Rather than accepting the piece-of-shit microwave that came with the rental unit, and continuing my lifelong luck of being at the right place at the right time, I fell into a random discount appliance store the day they were having a promotional "get this crap out of here" sale. I purchased a modest fridge and it came with a free microwave. I was single and working a lot as an hourly line cook, so this was perfect.

After a couple days, I realized the clock on the microwave was a few minutes behind the other several hundred clocks I had within sight. Look, this was the early 2000s. I didn't have a smartphone yet and not everything had been simplified into digital units, handheld devices, and streaming services. This was a small, two-bedroom joint. The kitchen and dining/living area was a common space. I had a clock on the wall above the couch. There was a clock on the wall in the kitchen covering the irrelevant phone jack. There was a clock on the oven. There was a clock on the VCR. There was a clock on the DVD player. There was an alarm clock on the side table for when I chose to sleep on the couch. I still occasionally wore a watch. My clamshell Nokia had a clock. There were clocks everywhere. Yet the one on the damn microwave, no matter how many times I reset it, was always a few minutes behind within a day or two.

Then I figured it out.

This masterpiece of cooking technology that was so valuable its merchants were giving it away for free had a bit of a glitch. Apparently, when you heated up food (you know, its one job), its clock would malfunction for the duration of cooking time. If it were 12:00 and you heated something for three minutes, the timer would ding ding ding but the clock would still read 12:00 as all the other clocks in my literal Times Square would have continued on to 12:03.

This.

Drove.

Me.

Mad.

Er, madder, I guess. But it forced me to realize something. For quite a few weeks, I would begrudgingly reset the clock. Then reset it again. Knowing the same thing was going to happen, I would insanely reset it again. It's all there—obsession, compulsiveness, stubbornness, unhealthy persistence—and this was just my battle against a digital clock on a microwave.

As I was just beginning to step into a recovery program and the buzz was all about acceptance, acceptance,

acceptance, one day it slapped me in the face. Accept it. Get over it. This machine's primary function isn't even to be a clock for crying out loud. *Accept it.*

FINALLY ACCEPTING

This is so ridiculously simple. As mentioned previously, so much of recovery is not easy, but simple. A freebie microwave forced me to see I could not control the world. That microwave made me acknowledge my ungiving drive to try to find different results from what is proven to be the same again and again and again. I don't have to like it, but I can agree with the world around me that this is the way it's going to be and move on with my life.

The day you take the world around you at face value and accept things for what they are, a part of your soul shines in a way it never has. By relinquishing an attempt at having total power, you are given a much more powerful gift—the strength of internal happiness.

With a good handful of sober years under my belt, I stopped and looked over my shoulder. I saw a guy that decided to live honestly and in sobriety on September 29, 2005. And I watched him remove that evil from his life and then continue living the same way he always had. Safely. Securely. Unthreatening. I had so suppressed the irrational desires to conquer *the* world that I no longer had the desire to conquer *my* world. I was fine doing the bidding of others. I was fine with missing so much time with my family. I was fine with being average, with being tired, with being just okay. I was fine with simply being fine.

The story of recovery continues here. Getting rid of the booze, getting rid of the mind and mood altering substances is not the end all. There is a needed self-exploration of *why*. Why do we think the way we do? Why do we seek comfort in behaviors that eventually hurt us? Why is our self-awareness and our perception so skewed? In my case, "Why am I in this grand competition? Who am I competing against? What spoils go to the victors? Is there even a victor?"

I came to terms with being wrong, with having a completely blown-out-of-proportion ego, with realizing I'm just an extra face in the crowd for so many other people.

The biggest realization of all? Accepting that not everyone approved of my antics. This might be common sense to many. For me, it was slashing through my chest and pulling my heart from me.

And it was liberating. When I realized I was no longer responsible for other people's thoughts, what a day it was. Discovering that I need not influence nor care about opinions, preferences, and functions—man, you talk about a burning bush moment. This was Sherwood Forest going up in flames as the poor me was given a fortune of freedom to move forward fearlessly. Freedom to walk off the imaginary field of the pretend competition regardless of what the nonexistent scoreboard said. Walking away meant I won. I won another day. I won another reprieve on life.

I could go forward and do what I liked. I could live how I wanted to live. I could make my decisions based on my interests and my curiosity.

I did it. I didn't have to compromise who I was just to be friends with the dope dealer. There could be people I didn't necessarily care for, but I didn't have to hate them. I taught myself to look at other people's points of view. I grew empathy. I nurtured my own personal humanity. My taste in music expanded. My interests changed. I saw more light and experienced more warmth when I finally gave up what I realized was not serving me.

For many, the first couple years of sobriety are indeed the most exciting. There's a lot going on. But also, if it makes sense and logical, like-minded colleagues can agree, it can involve some "time to live" moments. In my experience, after a year or so when self-inventories are done, self-awareness is honest, and motives are clear, it can be a time of great change. Jobs, relationships, the pursuit of true happiness.

BIGGEST CHANGE OF ALL

Have I said before how much I enjoyed my time in the restaurant industry and the lifelong friends I made? I can't say that enough. But for the uninitiated, just imagine being submerged in an environment where outside of the daily grind and business demands it is a nonstop, endless competition of who can be the biggest asshole. And this competition is being held with those that are on your very own team! And it isn't judged fairly or objectively—might makes right. The hierarchy determines the outcome of this glorious competition.

Wait a minute ... are we back in a competition?

I'm pulling in extra stress. I'm sacrificing my well-being, mentally and physically, for what I see as necessary. I trust the team I have developed but at the same time have got to outwork them all or my worth is questioned. Worse, I tell my family goodbye on Thursday and see them again Monday night.

Is this why I got sober?

Is this the happy ending?

I felt stepping back and saying "this is too much" was a sign of failure, a huge weakness. The stress of the job was in fact real, but the extra cherries I kept throwing on top were killing me. I began to think of leaving restaurants five years before I finally made the move. Because it is easier to sit comfortably in a self-made pile of shit than it is to get up, clean yourself off, and bet on yourself. Wait a minute ... isn't *this* familiar also?

The drugs and alcohol made this harder to see. A sober mind made it painfully obvious. Yes, it is important to have a career. Yes, it is important to have a sense of self-worth. But it is more important to have quality of life. Spiritual balance. Peace. Purpose.

I mentioned my family and their careers. It might seem like I was doing this comparison, this competition that I speak against here, but it wasn't superficial. I saw them living with intent and with purpose. They were making an impact and having a positive influence on those they interacted with. Surely there are parts of all jobs that are unfavorable, but do the positives make it worth it? Are you truly proud of what you are, what you are becoming, and any kind of legacy you are creating?

Are.

You.

Happy?

There are a lot of external factors that trick us: internet mumbo jumbo, corporate structures, things that feed on our egos that can misdirect us.

Here are a few realities: Being busy does not equal success. A company's success isn't *your* success. And I was intrigued by the simple yet powerful quote from the great American philosopher Tracy Marrow: "Attention does not mean success." In a time of social media likes, influencers, and viral content, this sort of attention doesn't necessarily bring the success and happiness you seek. It is a lie. A lie to keep the machine running, to keep the hamsters running on the wheel, to keep the hierarchy in place.

Remember me talking about having a hole that needs to be filled? Acceptance can at times be the shovel, with gratitude for what you haven't been paying attention to that matters—I mean really matters—being the filler.

We exist in addiction. We live in sobriety. We are forever in recovery. That is acceptance.

"It is okay to celebrate the antihero. It is not okay to become him."

CHAPTER 21

HEROES AMONG US

We all love a good hero. Especially the larger-than-life icons we are drawn to admire or emulate. They are super beings. Living immortals among us. The Hollywood action hero that avenges evil. The basketball star that drops fifty points and single-handedly wins games. Hell, even that damn animated lion that became king. Powerful. Inspirational. Motivating.

We even love a good antihero. That villain thwarting the hero's every move.

Fearless. Undaunting. Awe inspiring. And a corrupt, misleading investment. The movie eventually ends. It was just a character. The star athlete is attended to by practically futuristic medicinal procedures and puts in the work that isn't always as spotlighted as the success. The illustrator puts his pencils down.

To absorb abstract principles and use them as tools for inspiration or wisdom is one thing. To adopt personas and expect your own personal Hollywood ending is blindly foolish. We know this, yet we'll just go ahead and give it a shot anyhow.

LARGER THAN LIFE

Another hero dynamic is what I refer to as "those bullshit Nike ads." Don't get me wrong, I love me some kicks. But as an athlete, I took these ads, these sayings, and these propagandas to heart. As a swimmer I embraced Speedo and Arena ads with a vengeance, with their classic "what does not kill you makes you stronger" concept. I didn't just look at these and smile. I clipped them out and plastered them everywhere. Beyond pieces for inspiration, I placed myself in a nonexistent jungle, claiming to be alpha lion to an animal kingdom that no one even knew they were included in.

I wasn't as larger than life as I imagined. I was in an ego-driven mental state. I had put myself on an elevated, unrealistic pedestal where I legitimately held myself in the highest regard of a world-class athlete. I was good. In fact, I was above average despite having average size, average talent, and average strength. I achieved certain levels of success due to a little hard work and determination. The way I carried myself and the way I figured the world viewed me, you would've thought I was the second coming—well, I guess the first coming—of Michael Phelps. And yes, for those keeping score, this all started in my early teens, which was way before any regular drug or alcohol use.

Then there is the intrigue and forbidden admiration associated with the antihero.

I liked the Detroit Pistons. Know why? Because they were the Bad Boys. Because they fought. Bill Laimbeer, the NBA bully. Dennis Rodman, the biggest outcast and freak the NBA had ever seen. Why did I like these guys? Because they were outlaws. And more importantly, no one else around me liked them.

Brian Bosworth played football for the University of Oklahoma—a college I cared nothing about—but this dude was being plastered all over the media. California surfer good looks. Beast of a physique. Mohawks. Different-colored hair at times. I didn't know too much, but I knew this guy was gaining clout as a badass. And I freaking loved it.

For swimming I was fond of Melvin Stewart, a local favorite, and Pablo Morales, my sentimental favorite. Then there was the stud, Matt Biondi. Yeah, I know I'm dating myself with these Olympian swimmers. But while you're googling these dudes, look up Nelson Diebel also. An Olympic gold medalist and world's record holder, he was also viewed by the swimming world as an overachieving outlaw. His wrist was repaired with metal rods due to a stupid daredevil mishap. Ending up in boarding school after he turned to drugs and destructive behavior following his parents' divorce, Diebel fumbled his way into a swimming career. And not only did I find sanctity and inspiration in his story, I immersed myself with it. This dude is from a fractured family. This dude does the opposite of what everyone tells him. This dude really, really misbehaves.

It is okay to celebrate the antihero. It is not okay to become him.

Not only the "real world" but also popular culture entices us to go to the dark side. Movies bring the outlaws and the bad guys. It was all just so appealing to me. The character Chong Li from *Bloodsport* was made to be hated—an evil, corrupt competitor in the movie's MMA-esque tournament. He became my hero. You can't deny Val Kilmer's portrayal of Doc Holliday in *Tombstone*, but I did more than just admire. I wanted to become them. I wanted to feel that unabashedly self-initiated power and unapologetic bravado. I wanted people to fear me in the way Doc Holliday was feared. I wanted to live as fearlessly as Doc and kill as coldheartedly and remorselessly as he did.

Just reading this now makes me think, WTF? It probably makes you think the same too.

THE REAL HEROES

If you remove expectations, quit being a shallow superficial asshole, and stop looking for capes and logos, heroes aren't hard to find. They're among us, living and breathing and striving with us.

I entered a meeting during my second go-around with AA and went through the opening motions: you take a seat, attention is called, there's a prayer, and the meeting is turned over to the chosen leader for the night.

"Hi, I'm Chris, and I'm an alcoholic."

The world fades away with my complete tunnel vision on this guy. I hear nothing, and I feel chills. I see nothing but him. As he continues with the ritualized openings, I remember.

I remember this same Chris running back and forth with me across the soccer fields of Pinewood Elementary. We played on several teams together in our earlier years for Grace Methodist Athletic Association.

I remember this same Chris running through the halls of Smith Junior High School. Although he was a year older than me, he was never too cool to talk to a friend from a younger grade. My seventh-grade and his eighth-grade year, we won the league championship representing Grace.

I remember this same Chris from three years later, when I was in tenth grade and he was in eleventh. He was dressed completely in black and no longer friendly and smiling. We'd reduced our interactions to head nods. I gave up soccer for swimming after that championship season and I had no clue what he was into.

Whatever it was, it didn't seem good. He looked emaciated. His hair was stringy and unkempt, and his clothes were adorned with upside-down crosses. There were rumors of debauchery and terror that surrounded him (that's the guy who did a how-to speech in Mrs. Furr's class on "How to Crucify a Baby"). I was in the bathroom one time, and he came in behind me. As I stood at the glorious urinal wall, he went into a stall. The sounds of clicks were heard, as if a small case was being opened and closed. I got out of there as quickly as possible; minimal shaking and no handwashing this time.

I remember this same Chris not graduating and seemingly disappearing. No big exit. No tragic saga. Just poof—one day he was gone.

Then I see this same Chris standing in front of me. Clean. Hair still a bit wild, but you can tell it's been washed. Still a skinny dude, but there's life in his face. He flashes a smile that I hadn't seen in close to twenty years. Although it was missing a few teeth from the last time I saw him, I can see the joy in that smile. The youth in it. The life back in it.

Had I seen this guy not knowing who he was, I would've looked down on him as a toothless-grin loser. Had I seen him perhaps a few years earlier, living on the street, I would have felt nothing for him. But after having addresses in several states, I found myself here, living in a city that had AA and NA meetings every hour and half hour from 7:00 a.m. to 10:00 p.m.—hundreds a day. And I am sitting in one of these meetings being led not only by an old friend, but by an old friend I saw go from bright and shining to dark and morbid. In that moment, I see him again. Smiling. Leading. Being respected for his experiences. Helping others.

I was blessed to be in this moment. Had this not happened, I might not have ever believed sobriety was possible. This Chris did not fit my idea of a hero. He did not fit the profile of what I thought success was. And here he was, saving my f'n life.

My streak of good fortune with timing put me in the same meeting where a man from my past, who would become my sponsor, was randomly speaking. It's almost like if you open your mind and seek the good in the world, the universe responds to what it is you need. Wow, imagine that, huh?

HERO NEXT DOOR

I found myself in this late meeting again on a Monday night. As I sit here years removed from that day, my memory of it being a Monday is held tight because Mondays were always speaker meetings.

We did the opening gig, said some stuff, and read some stuff. Andy was introduced and took his place behind the podium.

Andy was older than me, but I was trying hard to look past differences in age, sex, economic background, education, and any other smoke screens we indulge in as distractions that keep us blind to the similarities we share. I was an alcoholic and addict, built the same as a single mom living in poverty and addiction fifty years ago. Exterior factors might have an influence, but it is a screwed view of the world and not understanding our own feelings that is the core of who we are. In front of me on that Monday night, Andy was explaining this to me.

As I listened intently, I felt an appreciation for once again being at the right place at the right time. This guy, this AA celebrity, was touching my soul and telling *my* story to me. I just hadn't gotten to the recovery part, to the happy ending. He had shown me how our paths, our stories, years and a generation apart, were very much one and the same. I was in awe that he had flown in or however he had gotten here to share this with us. I imagined how great it must be for him to travel from meeting to meeting, city to city, state to state, and inspire those looking for help. I'm not gonna lie: I found myself imagining that one day my story of recovery and helping others would somehow land me on this celebrity speaking circuit.

There I go again, comparing and creating my own competition within my head. Remember, I'm not perfect and I wasn't cured. I'm still driven by competition, and if there were going to be a recovery hierarchy, I was shooting for the top.

The meeting ended with the usual hold hands and pray-hug your neighbor fanfare: "Hold on tight to the one next to you, he or she might be the one that saves your ass one day."

We slowly made our way outside, doing our best to abide by the 11:00 p.m. quiet ordinance laid out by the city. People formed cliques as normal, with our celebrity guest speaker being in the center of a buzz of people coming and going.

I approached Andy and thanked him. I wasn't sure of the protocol, and it was a little before selfies were a thing. I hadn't seen anyone else ask him for an autograph, so I did what I was told by my sponsor and several other AA members.

If you see someone that has what you want, ask them how to get it.

With the confidence of the school dweeb approaching the prom queen, I asked Andy if I could have his phone number. I figured I could at least say I tried after he said no. He surely had a lot of traveling to do and more speeches to give.

Well, this dweeb went home with the prom queen that night. Andy flashed an incredibly bright and genuine smile as he leaned on his red convertible, his Indiana Jones–style hat completing his Neil Young look. He stood up straight and wrote his number down for me.

Wow, I thought. This dude is really cool. I wonder if he drove this thing all the way from California? Or if he rented it from the airport? Or maybe he has a whole fleet of these around the country? This is getting exciting. I went home quite afire by what looked like a promising future and the giddiness of meeting such a big shot.

The next day I went back to the same 10:00 p.m. meeting. Beginning to open up, I shook more hands and tried to sneak up to circles to fit in. I felt welcomed. I didn't feel alone anymore. And, holy shit, Andy is here! That's cool, he must be spending a few days here before he travels on.

I made sure to say hello to Andy and did the handshake, the coffee tap, and the cigarette talks. Jesus, I never smoked as many cigarettes as I did my first year in recovery. I was still mesmerized by Andy—by the story he told, the hope he shared, the celebrity radiating off him. I've always been entranced by the pedestaled ones. But unlike the outcasts, thugs, and fantasy villains I had so desired to parallel my story with, I was standing with one I could really, really relate to on every level.

Then some reality began to settle. The next day, Andy was there again. The next day, Andy was there. The next day ... yep, again. I had to laugh at myself as the magician's trick revealed that—da-da-da-daaaaaaaa—Andy was, in fact, not a touring AA celebrity speaker. He actually lived about five miles from me.

This is what is important to recovery, and I was lucky enough to be ignorant about what was going on the night Andy got up to speak. It is imperative to abandon all previous methods of thinking. It is crucial to survival to not put up the walls and hide behind differences, but to look through barricades and find similarities in the core. The core is the spirit, the pride, the feelings, the fear, and the emotions. Deep, deep down, we addicts are all the same.

Had I known this old man simply lived in the Dilworth area (for those not familiar with Dilworth just ask yourself, does it sound like the poor side of town to you?!) and breathed the same Charlotte air as me, my ears might not have been open. For whatever reason, I deemed him as important, and I saw something special empowering me to listen. And he indeed turned out to be someone remarkably special to me. The answers are always there. The heroes are among us. We just need to quit looking for them in the form we want them to be, and embrace them in the form they need to be in for us.

I am a lucky man. Again, big props to the nondiscriminatory ways of addiction and to unexpected heroes.

"This isn't a dip your toes into the water and test the temperature. This is a headfirst plummet into the deep end.**"**

CHAPTER 22

MAKING AMENDS

When I finally got fired from Rafferty's, I handled it pretty, uh … not too well. And by "not too well" I mean I formed conspiracies against those that "got me fired," refusing to believe I got fired because I deserved it, begged for it, screamed for it from the mountaintop through my actions. By "not too well" I mean I used racial slurs against my main culprit and wished death upon his family members. There ended up being a fight in the following weeks with me losing a tooth and him receiving a few lumps as well. He didn't deserve the physicality he suffered. I totally deserved the punch in my mouth.

In the most coincidental turn of events, years later we ended up beside each other at a stoplight 103 miles north of where we worked together. We pulled over to an adjacent drugstore, got out of our cars, and talked. I was gifted the privilege of apologizing. We shook hands and did that half-man-hug thing. I admit that when I got out of the car, I thought I might be getting stabbed. But I knew I had to face the situation I had created.

Part of cleaning up our past is making amends. We are often instructed on the big ones we need to pursue at the beginning of the recovery process. Some we call "life amends," such as my need to stay sober not just for my sake but to remove that evil from the world. We owe institutions amends. We also have many amends that for reasons outside of our control will never be made. Deaths, separations, and lives moving on—all these can prevent face-to-face or direct outreach amends.

THE UNEXPECTED ONES

The best amends are the unexpected ones. When someone or something you have forgotten suddenly pops up, like pulling up next to them at a stoplight. There isn't time to form a script, there isn't a long drive for you to change your mind and turn around, and there isn't a written letter for you to tear up. You just speak from the heart. It's you, your surprised recipient, and your integrity and accountability.

The cool thing about making amends is they help with those wrecked connections. A burnt bridge cannot just be replaced, but sometimes the destination can be reached with a different route. My lifetime ban from Goucher has since been forgotten. A friend named Alice Kennedy helped remove all the Wanted Dead or Alive posters from the campus. The security team that was hired just to watch for my face on surveillance cameras retired. She informed me it was a nonissue and no one gives a damn about me. She wasn't as harsh as that, but man that's what my ego heard.

And believe it or not, I have gone back to many 7-Elevens. No drama. As long as I'm not running out the door with merchandise I didn't pay for, no one checks my name on the 7-Eleven Banned Consumer Database.

And just like not stealing hot dogs keeps me as inconspicuous as Elvis in Australia, I have visited many a property of Mecklenburg County. Again, if I'm not carrying drugs and weapons, being intoxicated and climbing on the roof, or parking my car in a hidden breezeway (I think I left that out the first time), no one really seems to mind that I came to eat lunch with my nephew on his birthday. I was even approved as a chaperone for my daughter's field trips. To a "normal," that isn't really that remarkable. To me, anytime before September 29, 2005, that was unthinkable. Hello world, I'm not afraid of you today.

GETTING STARTED

So where do you start? What amends do you need to make? What amends will you just have to pay forward because that face-to-face isn't possible?

You start at the beginning. You start with the most pain. This is a headfirst plummet into the deep end, not dipping your toes into the water to test the temperature. You start with the two or three biggest screwups you've had. The ones you hurt the most. Because they deserve it. Because they will be the most difficult. And because they will be the biggest relief from your soul. Like many stages on this journey, my experience with this was having a confidant talk you through these and walk along with you. Amends can be very sensitive for us, and they can be downright deadly if we make that plunge without knowing how to swim.

My first three amends were to be a relationship or friendship I had ruined, my mom, and my college. Three separate entities and all requiring different plans of attack. My mom was geographically the easiest to do. At this point of my recovery, I was back living in the old neighborhood. I was doing well in a modest little duplex despite the damn microwave. It was about three houses down from where one of those other Stooges lived, and I could see my parents' house from a couple of my windows. There was no excuse not get this one done.

I remember it vividly. It was around nine on a weekday morning. My dad had already left for work, and I'd attended an early AA meeting. I followed the advice given to me, told myself the things I needed to tell myself, and walked across the threshold I had crossed thousands of times before.

We exchanged cordial rhetoric, and my mom could tell I was holding back. I sat propped on the arm of their god-awful, patterned couch and my throat filled with that crushed feeling. As I spoke, it was more air than voice.

"I am an alcoholic and I am sorry," I said, looking right in her eyes. And although I still sat upon the floral cushioned throne, it was as if I were catapulted into a stratosphere of serene enlightenment. It was a sensory overload in a way I cannot accurately describe. It was intensely loud and silent at the same time. I had tunnel vision with rainbow kaleidoscope traces. My heart pounded, yet it stood still. I could smell every meal ever cooked in the adjacent kitchen and I could hear the grass growing outside. And all I wanted was for her to say something.

"I know you are. And all we want is for you to be happy."

Well, damn. What an anticlimactic letdown that was. But I learned a lesson that day. These amends, although great burdens we have carried for years, might not be the same earthshaking moment for the people and places we've hurt as it is for us. For me, this was a life-changing moment of cleansing. For my mom, it was an honest conversation with her baby boy. We continued a very cordial, loving conversation.

When I left the house, I assume she went about her usual daily business. When I crossed back over that threshold, it was the first time I did so as a free man. Once again, hello world. I am not afraid of you.

MANY, MANY OTHERS

On the other end of the spectrum, well beyond the view of my living room window, I owed Goucher College an apology and explanation. The hurdle of being 643 miles away was compounded by my lifetime ban. This is, as explained to me, when you employ a living amend. Although there were many individuals affected by my gross behavior, overall it was the institution that I violated and cheated.

I owed poor Miss Helen, the cleaning lady, countless apologies for the nightly mess I made. I owed the facilities apologies for the vandalism. I owed my fellow students apologies for everything from pointless bullying all the way to the late-night arson evacuation. Amy, I am sorry I set your door wreath on fire. I owed the professors apologies for wasting their time with someone that had no intention of taking their classes seriously.

How do you amend this? You never do it again. You never forget it. You don't dwell on it and wear it as a constant badge of regret, but you use it as a model of how to act. Take care of your environment. Respect those around you. Understand that we all have different likes, interests, causes, and purposes, and allow each other to flourish in our chosen direction. Support and love. Clean up your mess. Leave it the way you found it. Put the damn cart back, and let people know when you're turning.

The third of my top-priority amends was another that was out of reach. I didn't have to overcome an eight-hour drive, but both of us agreed that we shouldn't be around each other anymore. We had mutual and exclusive friends who also strongly urged this and well, even a few judges and lawyers thought the same way. So, how do I do this?

Write them a letter and have a common friend give it to them. Unload all your apologies and admit all your shortcomings. Do not blame. Do not make excuses. Do not point out perceived thoughts of how they also screwed up. Unload your guilt and shame. What if the friend chooses not to deliver it? What if it is never read? What if it is shared among a large group and is laughed at? It doesn't matter. This is your soul being cleansed. This is you emptying the past so you can build a future. This is the proverbial cleaning of your house and yard despite the appearance of the houses around you. This is for *you* and *you* only. Unload. Release. Live.

NEVER DONE

The amends are never done. You'll run into people you have long forgotten. Handle it.

You'll have people bring up stuff long forgotten. Address it. Sean, I am sorry I stole your seat at Larry's.

You can't tell people their feelings are not valid; they are *their* feelings, not yours. If you did wrong, correct it. Holding on to transgressions corrupts our soul. It buries our good and it can unleash in us a catalyst of why we drank and drugged in the first place. We are not perfect, but we must strive. Where we used to give up and ignore, now we acknowledge and trudge through.

My wife and children have never seen me in active addiction, but they did see me addicted to my work.

The tools and principles learned while making amends are still incredibly relevant. When you screw up, admit it. Take accountability for your wrongs. Don't capitalize on anyone else's faults. Their wrongdoings, although frustrating and at times painful, are not for you to clean. You fix you. That's the way it works. Apologize and move on.

And the living amends? That continues forever. Everything I ever did to hurt someone, to insult and manipulate, has to go away and that behavior need never return. It's an amazing thing. Focus on yourself and clean up your energy and behavior, and the world around you will improve. The universe is indeed living and breathing, so breathe good into it.

I learned a solid foundation for making amends with my "big three." You're not always going to get a resounding shower of appreciation. Perhaps none will be given at all. It isn't a blame game or a justification. It is a display, an honest unveiling, of a self-inventory where you come clean for your moments of infringing on others.

It isn't up to you if it will be well received. It isn't up to you if it will evoke an apology in your direction when you feel you deserve one. Amends are not closing the door. Rather, they are keeping the door open and removing all dangerous obstacles. We don't "do" amends, we "live" amends. Amends provide confidence moving forward. We are not programmed to be angelic, but we must atone when we hurt others.

We are now armed and loaded with compassion, integrity, and accountability with a more accurate perspective of who and what we are in our world. These personality awakenings are tools we never chose to use before. These are tools that improve our understanding of our surrounding world and improve that surrounding world itself.

Making amends makes us better; living them makes us stronger.

❝ You can't be anything to anyone if you don't work on yourself from the inside out and the outside in. ❞

CHAPTER 23

A BETTER VERSION

Tonight was special. My former restaurant was celebrating thirty years of success while hosting a fundraiser dear to the community's heart.

It was special for Drew, the new chef spearheading his first major event, and it was special for me because I'd spent eighteen years laboring for this company. Now I was no longer part of the team. I was four months removed from being a restaurant worker. A cook. A chef. *The* executive chef. One of the boys. And it was weird. In my civilian gear, I schmoozed with a crowd of regulars I had fed and conversed with across the bar or table side for years—long enough to get a newborn through high school.

I spoke with Chef Drew many times. Hung out with the kitchen crew. Those guys in their impeccable whites with high hats and kerchiefs, and me in the clothes I usually reserve for minor traffic court appearances. They let me join in. It was fun. It was emotional. It was my life for a very, very long time.

Somehow, the owner, John Love—the Man of Love—managed to shake three hands at once, hug strangers, direct the staff, and still have enough time for me. More like a brother-father-friend than a boss, leaving this dude out of my daily life was one of the hardest parts about leaving the restaurant. But he understood. We hugged, I thanked him for inviting me, and then we did that awkward crap where we started telling each other how awesome the other one is. I swear he might've started to cry, but I didn't. There were onions on the nearby pasta station that might've gotten to me.

Three hours of laughs, hugs, axe throwing, and more laughing flew by. I was way past my curfew and needed to get home. On my way out I passed one of the dining areas and saw my world, except there was one thing missing.

I wasn't in it.

A PROUD MOMENT

Chef Drew stood among a dozen gleefully relieved cooks and staff, *his* staff, and they were taking a traditional post–big event picture. The smiles were genuine, but as much as they glowed with pride at their work, they also screamed with relief at it being over. Mission complete.

I remember that joy. Standing there in that two-second moment in time, the rush of performing and the sense of accomplishment registered in my taste buds like Grandma's roast beef. Except I was no longer sitting at the table, and in that instant I was jealous. "How come y'all never took pictures when I was here?" I yelled at the group, knowing we took pictures all the damn time.

But the jealousy quickly faded, and I was proud. Proud of Drew. Proud of the crew. As they unhugged and made their way back to the kitchen, I pointed at the crew one by one. "I hired you! And I hired you! And I hired you three times!" Truth be told, I'd hired most of the staff except two who were already there when I came on board in 2008. I gave Drew one last hug, and that one was where I felt it all. It was the final release of my hold on this kitchen; the passing of the torch, with the circle of life complete. Operations were now firmly cradled in his arms.

Drew credits me endlessly for being a mentor to him. I tell him all the time he was the perfect student—humble, with an eagerness to learn and the desire to be better. He's calm beyond his years and very rational and accepting of the world around him. He is grateful for what he has and can keep the focus on what is important. If he wasn't the perfect student, I would have been worthless as a mentor. You can't teach the unwilling. You can't learn from the unwilling.

I pride myself on having the uncanny gift of "right place, right time." In a universe fourteen billion years old, on a rotating ball of dirt five billion years old, in a country a quarter of a century old, in a state two hundred thirty years old, in a business three decades old, we were both exactly where we needed to be, when we needed to be there, at the exact same time.

In a moment of reflection about that night, I saw a parallel with Drew and me. At one time he was a protégé, and now he was my equal and even superior. What's more, he met his lady working together and they started a family. He had grown immensely.

BEFORE ADDICTION'S GRASP

When Drew started down a path of daily highs, his wake-up call came in the form of a close friend overdosing and not making it. It crumbled him to the core and made him look in the mirror and decide he didn't want the same demise. He didn't want to end up like that.

Heck, he may have thought the same thing about me, even though I was his mentor and his golden key to the kitchen one day. He had the sense I didn't have at his age to see reality and make better choices.

He had to go away to be found. Drew put his life on pause because he knew he'd gone too far in the wrong direction and it was time to change. He developed a positive support system instead of friends of convenience. Friends of substance, not just Lowest Common Denominators. Not only did he know the difference between right and wrong, but he would stand and fight for his morals.

One of the greatest gifts I received in sobriety was the opportunity to see Drew go through it. With Drew, it was amazing and I let him know it. His progress from where he started to where he is now is impressive. I like to fancy myself as a success, but here he is, over ten years ahead of me in terms of what I had accomplished at his age. I'm almost old enough to be his father, but Drew is my contemporary. I'm glad to see him with his family and excelling in his career.

The journey of addiction and recovery sees no age, and it sees no demographic. It swoops in and runs its course. It either runs you into the grave or it runs you to the point of asking for help.

Drew asked for help. The sooner you get help, the more time you have to enjoy life living clean and free. As I planned to step away from the industry, I confided in him before letting anyone else know. I am old. I am tired. I am missing too much. I've got to make this change for me. With his best interests in mind, I looked at him and pleaded with him not to get old. Time is too precious and goes by too quickly, which is a lesson I had to come to terms with myself. Get sober to live. Get sober to flourish. Enjoy life fully.

I admire that about him. Drew being a better version of himself has helped me continue to focus on being a better version of me.

THE MIRACLE OF YOU

Don't believe in miracles? I do. I've seen them.

You get sober and decide to live the way *you* want to live. If you remove the alcohol and drugs as a way of coping and do nothing else to improve your life, your external and internal being, then you might as well keep getting zooted.

If you plan on excelling and including others and living out dreams but know your -isms and -tions have you living a miserable, unmanageable existence, then go ahead and stay in the gutter. Either way, don't get your hopes or the hopes of others up.

Being a better version of you is where it begins. You can't be anything to anyone if you don't work on yourself from the inside out and the outside in. Your perception is your reality.

Take. Take with you everything that you saw wrong with any arrangement or relationship. Take with you the image of what you thought it should and could be and remember the contrast of what it was. Take the energy you had and remember what it was like. Bottle it like summertime-caught fireflies and bask in the light. Learn from the insight of what could have been better.

Create. Discover the reality you had sought. Remember the wrongs that frustrated you, the communication breakdowns, the nonvisible but very much constricting walls. Release the fireflies, and allow the glow to fill the new world you find yourself in. Indulge in the freedom the previous situations didn't allow by creating something better.

Remember. Above all else, never become the person or institution from which you fled. Do not speak to those in ways you did not like being spoken to. Do not treat others in ways you did not like to be treated. Do not create rules and boundaries for others that you grew to resent because it inhibited who you wanted to be. Remove the negatives of which you encountered. Give to the world the opportunities and respect you felt you were robbed of. Do this with a sober mind, and do this to live even better.

LIVING SOBER

I have hung out, on separate occasions, with members of Cypress Hill and the Kottonmouth Kings. If you don't know who they are, go ahead and hit the google real quick—I'll wait.

I know, right? And I have the pictures to prove it! But I was *there* for the moment. For the fellowship of music, not just as an excuse to get trashed. I was there to *live*. The band (hed) p.e., a personal favorite, has also gone through quite a metamorphosis. From songs driven by meth binges and strip club fiascos to a mellow, reggae punk vibe, the band as an entity has made necessary changes for a higher quality of life. And although they still might indulge in cannabis and alcohol, I don't have to when I listen to their music. Because yeah, I became friends with a rock star *after* I quit being a drunken bum.

Self-respect is cool, but have you zip-lined through a rainforest? I did once I became sober.

WrestleMania. Spur-of-the-moment, worry-free drives to the beach. Beautiful vacations. My oldest child is seven years younger than my sobriety, so baw chicka baw baw, that happens sober also.

But you know what else? When my mom went one-on-one with a sedan and came up a little short in that battle, I was able to drive to the hospital and be totally present with her. I've been able to have family and friends over and not be embarrassed about the smell or holes in the walls. I've been to weddings, funerals, and birthday parties. And I've been really, really happy.

I have looked at myself in the mirror, with my momma's big ole nose and my daddy's bottom row of crooked teeth. I see a man whose worth I questioned for years. Damn, I questioned his existence. I questioned his will. I look into the mirror, sober, and I am my parents' son.

And I'm happy.

"Challenge yourself, your values, your worth based on who you were yesterday, who you are today, and who you strive to be tomorrow. "

CHAPTER 24

LIVING LIFE FULLY

We as human beings are constructed for greatness. There are workers and there are leaders. Some are stronger than others, some are smarter. But we all are 100% able to have a personal greatness that we should work toward. We should never fear failure, for failure is nothing but another opportunity to get it right. To do it better.

Live within reality and live within means, but Jesus Christ, man, shoot for the f'n stars. The younger this lesson is learned, the better. I see Drew and others like him, who get this and embrace this. I see my children building their personalities, and I pray they figure it out earlier than when I did.

Happiness really isn't a destination; it's a state of mind. It's a peaceful existence. It is *living with a purpose.*

I heard for a lifetime how money isn't everything. It also took me that long to believe it. Money isn't everything. Creating your own life stream is everything. Touching another human being's soul is everything. The smile of your child, the approval of your parent, or giving your hand when someone reaches out—*that* is everything. Right now is everything. All we have is what is laid before us—the air in our lungs, the vision in our eyes, and the beats in our hearts. Do not waste time living falsely. Do not waste time working for other people's goals.

DEFINE YOU

Do not waste time compromising who you are for the sake of someone else. We are destined for greatness, each one of us. The level of greatness, the definition of what that greatness is, it all relies on you, the individual. I cannot say it enough and I will say it until the day I die:

Do not let the world define you. You must define the world around you.

Play by the rules. Break them if they need to be broken for the greater good of all. Live up to commitments. Always help, and always love. Steer your life in the direction you want it to go. Always believe in yourself. Never, never, never give up.

About fifteen years into sobriety, I realized giving up the dope and booze was indeed actually the easy part. Getting off my ass and finally deciding to live, finally deciding to be great, and finding a way to be the person I was supposed to be the whole time—that's the hard part.

We ultimately owe it to ourselves—and we can also lump in there our parents, our spouses, our children, our dogs, our favorite teacher—to be the absolute best and brightest shining star that we are meant to be.

There's a line from a Blind Melon song, "Change," about how you might as well die if you stop dreaming. There is a major discrepancy between living and existing. Drug addicts and alcoholics, we exist. We even exist as functional, job-holding, churchgoing, family-loving people. But it's an existence where we have become slaves to substance in a self-imprisoned world. The keys of self-exploration, honesty, and sobriety are well within reach, just not spiritually attainable.

To *live*, to grow, to dare, to dream, and to explore fearlessly, requires that you take the chance by betting on yourself, believing in yourself, and investing in yourself. None of this comes about playing it safe. None of this comes from existing. None of this comes from a world of complacency.

The *life* we deserve to have, the life we are destined to have, and the life we owe it to ourselves to have is right there for us each to take. We just have to get off our asses and reach out and take it.

EMBRACING YOU

Know your worth. Know your value. Know you don't simply fit in; you choose where you want to be and how you want to be. At any given time, you can elevate who you are by simply choosing to do so.

The energy is there. We can work endlessly day in and day out because it is comfortable, because it is safe. Put that effort into what *you* believe. Work on *you*. Your projects, your passions. Make that competition with yourself a healthy one. It isn't about excess; it's about quality.

You thought I was tripping about those shopping carts, huh? Build a reputation of doing what is morally right. We attract what we emit.

Challenge yourself, your values, your worth based on who you were yesterday, who you are today, and who you strive to be tomorrow—not on a coworker, not on a fictional character, but on *you*. This is healthy. Trust me, if a plant could water itself, it would, and this is how we self-nurture. That lion that gets up to run for food doesn't wait for the domesticated dog bowl. He goes and gets it. He finds a way. Merely surviving is not living. Flourishing, growing, improving—that's living. You will see that it isn't a light at the end of the tunnel. Instead, it's a light that is emitting from your very own being. There isn't a pot of gold at the end of the rainbow. The rainbow is indeed the treasure within you—your brilliance, your purpose, your life.

Work on constantly improving your fellowship with those around you. That is what is important. Your position in a company isn't important, nor is your income or the shoes on your feet. What is your worth? It is what you make it to be by the actions you take, and how you leave whatever you touch better than it may have been before. That is worth. That is value. That is living life fully.

It's a popular knuckle tattoo: "Stay True." It can also be found in countless songs and even on tacky made-for-bathroom placards, but the tattoo culture means a little more to me. Once the sobriety is found, once denial is overcome, once an ability to balance our fears and hold ourselves accountable is gained, we are left with the person we should be. Our potential is increased, our visions are clearer, and our dreams are now more realistic. To not be who we are meant to be is not staying true. We are cheating ourselves. In all of our worldly travels, with all the thousands of people we will meet, there is one person that we must have an undying loyalty toward. And that person for each of us is ourselves. No more self-sabotaging. No more self-denying.

As we embrace sobriety, but more importantly as we are human beings, we owe it to the world to be exactly who we want to be. We owe it to ourselves. We owe it to the innocent child we once were with a headful of dreams. We owe it to the goals a younger, pre-self-destructive addict put on hold. That is the ultimate truth. No more hiding, no more excuses, no more denial. The mask is removed, and now you can stay true to who you really are.

Without our shackles, we are stronger than ever. Limitless. Clean. Clear. Now we drive with purpose. Now we drive with vision. And with the same undeniable will that we used to chase our demons, we can now chase our dreams.

Unafraid.

Unrestricted.

And UnLoaded.

ACKNOWLEDGMENTS

First and foremost, I want to acknowledge that I believe in a God of my understanding. I believe there is a plan for us all, and this is just a small part of mine.

To Fabi and Sherré, thank you for panning through a much different, far more vulgar first draft and pulling the message out that needed to be shared.

Thank you to John Love for showing me how to treat people. Blame all of this on Nicole Ross. She lit the fire.

For Nancy Lee Lively Payne and Cynthia Furr. You two will live forever in the hearts and voices of your students.

Judy Corbett ... I finally did it.

My mom and dad, thank you isn't enough. You are the perfect parents for me. I tested you beyond reason, and you were firm in your faith and constantly believed I'd find my way. I think I just might have after all. My beautiful Momma, I love you so much. And Dad, you are the greatest man I have ever known.

Tonya and Nicki also, I gave you so many reasons to give up on me and you never did. No one has ever had better sisters.

Sean Walker, the definition of a best friend.

My Goucher family and the mighty GMS. Rafferty's. Red Rocks Cafe. Jjrs. Starmount and even Candlewyck. Punk Rock Steve. Jim McDonough. Drew Pierce. Bill Lassiter. CPCC. One Eye D. Olympic High School. Mecklenburg Aquatic Club. The McLeod Center. Chris and Andy. The 10:00 group. Craig Newton, I'm still digging pretty holes, brother. Master Barber Kenny Tucker for keeping those lines straight. Kelsea McCree and Family Tradition Tattoo for the free tattoos that come with paid therapy. And so many more people and places. I believe we as individuals are a composite of everyone we have ever met. Thank you all for making me who I am. If you were to judge a man's wealth by the company he keeps, I'd be the richest in all the land.

My love, Jackie. You deserve your own book. Thank you for pushing me when I need to be pushed. You are stronger than anyone I know. Thank you for allowing me to bet on myself. Funny what came out of a little pizza date, huh? Also thank you for being way hotter than your twin. I love you endlessly in ways in which I haven't the words.

And to Danny and Suhu (and way too many others) ... I miss you. We all do.

AUTHOR BIO

Forever a Carolina kid, Jamie Weatherly was born and spent most of his life in Charlotte, NC. He claims Baltimore as his second home, with a few past addresses across the South East. Naturally gifted at writing and storytelling from a young age, Jamie made a series of horrible and life-threatening decisions to have more interesting stories to tell. With a significant chapter of his life spent in the restaurant industry, including a stint as head chef, Jamie's stories gained intricate details and flavors. A pivotal moment in Jamie's life occurred on September 29, 2005, marking the beginning of his journey towards sobriety. Fueled by a profound passion for his own recovery, he now feels compelled to share his story of hope and resilience. Through his experiences, Jamie aims to inspire everyone, especially those grappling with addiction, to embrace a life lived authentically, purposefully, and with unwavering intent.

Mark Hanson Photography

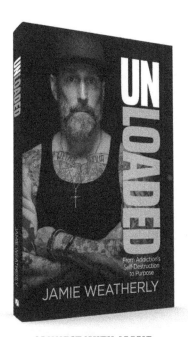

CONNECT WITH JAMIE:

JamieWeatherlyUnLoaded

To order books in bulk or ask questions, connect with
Jamie directly at: JDW929@jamieweatherly.com

LOG ON TO:

JamieWeatherly.com
For updates on appearances, speaking, and book signings

Printed in the USA
CPSIA information can be obtained
at www.ICGtesting.com
LVHW050830240624
783783LV00010B/22